*Growing
In All
The Right
Places*

Growing In All The Right Places

Joanne Putnam

Growing In All The Right Places

By Joanne Putnam

© 2000 Joanne Putnam

All Scripture quotations in this book are from the King James Version of the Bible unless otherwise identified.

All rights reserved. No portion of this publication may be reproduced, stored in an electronic system, or transmitted in any form or by any means, electronic, mechanical, photocopy, recording, or otherwise, except for the inclusion of brief quotations in a review or article, without the prior permission of the author.

Putnam, Joanne.
    Growing In All The Right Places
      1. Women—Religious life.   2. Women—Conduct of life.
1. Title
BV4527.P87   2000   284.8'43

Printed in the United States of America by
Morris Publishing • 3212 East Highway 30 • Kearney, NE 68847
1-800-650-7888

Table of Contents

Introduction
One
Vessels of Honor 11
Two
Our Search For Significance 19
Three
He didn't Lift Us Up To Let Us Down 23
Four
The Ugly Duckling 33
Five
The Cinderella Syndrome 39
Six
For Bitter or Better 57
Seven
Treasures of the Heart 73
Eight
Knit Pickers or Knit Fixers 87
Nine
Returning To Fist Love 93
Ten
Love Languages 99
Eleven
The Honeymoon Is Over 107
Twelve
Preparing Children For Life 113

Thirteen
Blueprints For a Happy Home 123
Fourteen
Blessing Your Children 131
Fifteen
Prayer Makes the Difference 141
Sixteen
Study To Show Yourself Approved 149
Seventeen
Spiritual Growth Journal 165
Eighteen
Leaders are Readers 169
Nineteen
For Those Tears 175
Twenty
Image Makers 179

A Special Note of Thanks

First I would like to thank God for helping me put into writing many of the principles He has taught me through the years. My desire is to continue to grow spiritually, for in Him, I am complete.

I would like to thank my husband, Reverend John Putnam, for his ardent support through the years. His loving kindness has smoothed away many rough edges in my life and helped me to become a woman God can use.

I would like to thank Reverend Aaron Soto for his many hours of editing and gentle critiquing. His insights and suggestions were extremely beneficial.

I would like to thank my daughter, Amy Grinnell, for taking time to preview and edit. Not once did she try to correct the way I told a story or discount anything she read!

I would like to extend special thanks to Diana Guerin for graciously allowing me to use her printer.

I especially want to thank the many dear friends, brothers and sisters in Christ, who not only encouraged me to keep on writing, but put their words into action as they daily prayed for me.

Introduction

The older I get, the more I understand the parable Jesus taught regarding the sower. In Mark 4, Jesus tells the story of a sower who went out to sow seeds. He described, in detail, the four types of ground that the seed fell on: the wayside, the stony ground, the thorny ground and the good ground.

He told His disciples that the wayside ground was so hard packed that when the seed fell the birds quickly devoured it. The stony ground was where the seeds sprouted quickly, but grew only shallow roots, so they soon withered and died. The thorny ground was where thorns and thistles choked the sprouts out. Then there was the good ground that yielded fruit and increased.

His disciples didn't fully understand the spiritual significance of this parable, so Jesus explained it further. He told them that the sower is the person who sows God's word. The ground represents the heart of man and it's spiritual condition. He went on to explain that some seed is sown by the wayside. These are those who hear God's truth but Satan soon snatches it away and it has no effect on their lives. Then there are people whose hearts are stony. When they first hear God's word, they are excited about it. They grow for a while but their roots never get a stronghold. When persecution comes or they encounter a difficult situation in their life, they burn out. They just disappear. The third type of heart is like thorny ground. As they begin to grow and face the day to day challenges of life, they are choked out. Instead of trusting God to meet their material needs, their time is spent seeking after the things of the world rather than the things of God.

Then Jesus talked about those whose hearts were compared to good ground: those who heard God's word and allowed it to grow deep into the fabric of their life. Those who cultivated their heart, weeding out the things of life that distracted them from the things of God. Those who allowed God's Holy Spirit to take control and lead them as they fed and watered their spirit daily in His presence.

When we give our heart to God, and are reborn in Him, we are a new creation. We are not born into Christ full-grown, we are a baby that has a lot of growing to do!

It is to that end that this book was written. Some chapters will cultivate the soil of your heart. Some chapters will water what is already growing there. Some chapters will plant new seeds of thought while others will help you identify weeds that need to be destroyed before they choke out the life of the Spirit of God. Some chapters may even seem like manure! At first they may seem abrasive or offensive, but in time, they provide the necessary nutrients to nourish the heart of good soil that brings forth, some thirty, some sixty and some one hundred fold!

My desire is to help *you* grow in all the right places!

Chapter One
Vessels of Honor

"But in a great house there are not only vessels of gold and of silver, but also of wood and of earth; and some to honour, and some to dishonour" (II Timothy 2:20).

If I asked you what a vessel is, what would you tell me? The dictionary tells us that a vessel is a utensil designed to hold dry or liquid ingredients. It's primary function is simply to hold something. Vessels have been mainstays in homes throughout the ages. They have always been *extremely* important.

If I asked you to think of yourself as a "vessel," what vessel would you choose to be? A china tea cup? A tea pot? An iron skillet? A thermos bottle? I've had some people tell me they were a "cracked pot!"

In every geological dig, the first thing archeologists look for are the vessels the people used. Holman's Bible Dictionary says that pottery is like the fingerprints of a culture. Archeologists can pinpoint the nation, tribe and specific time period that people lived in, according to the style and materials used in their vessels. The Bible mentions several types of vessels: stone, alabaster, wood, silver, gold, glass, baskets, wine jugs, animal skins, and the most widely used and cheapest of vessels were the earthenware vessels made of clay.

Vessels are just as important today as they were thousands of years ago. They may be made of different materials today: aluminum, plastic, stainless steel, or Styrofoam, but they serve the same basic purpose: they hold things. We have never lost our need for them.

Have you ever been told your water would be turned off for a period of time? What was the first thing you did? If you are like most people, you gathered everything you could find to fill up with water, including your bathtub.

In the United States, we are very fortunate to have a good, clean water supply. Many countries have a very limited water supply. A German friend of mine went to Malaysia to visit her in-laws for the first time. She wanted to take a cool bath after their long flight and when she went into the bathroom, she found that someone had already filled the tub with water. She took a refreshing bath and went to her room to get dressed when she heard a blood-curdling scream from her Mother-in-law! It didn't take Barbara long to realize that she had taken a bath in the entire days water supply!

When we moved to Germany to serve as missionaries several years ago, we sent over one hundred boxes through the mail. We had to pay for every ounce of goods we shipped, so I was very selective in what we sent. We had a couple of rummage sales and weeded through all of our belongings so we would send only the items that we considered most valuable. I got rid of all my plastic butter bowls, and artificial whipped topping bowls. You know, the kind of containers you put leftovers in. The things that if mold ends up growing in them, you don't mind throwing them out or sending them to school with your child for a science experiment! Certainly they weren't worth the cost of postage to ship them to Germany. And it was true… as far as money was concerned. But when I arrived and didn't have them, I found myself regretting having thrown them out! The Germans didn't sell margarine in tubs at that time, and plastic storage bags were not readily available like they are in the states. I realized that circumstances can quickly change the value of things! Those cheap little "vessels" were valuable to me after all!

"Vessels" have always held "high" significance in the Bible. There were vessels to wash in, cook in, store food in, and serve in. There were even vessels to keep tears in. Vessels were specifically designed and crafted for particular purposes. We see in the building of the Tabernacle, that great pains were taken to make the vessels that were to be used by the Priests.

God used vessels in one of the first recorded miracles found in the Bible. II Kings 4: 1-7 tells the story of the prophet Elijah and a widow woman whose two sons were to be sold to pay her husband's debts. Elijah asked her what she owned that was of value. She replied that she had no money but she had a little pitcher of oil. He told her to send her sons and collect all the vessels they could borrow. She was to fill the vessels with the oil from her little cruise of oil and sell it to pay her debts. The oil flowed from vessel to vessel until there were no more vessels available, and then it stopped. There was money enough to pay her husband's debt and keep the family for many years to come.

Jesus used vessels in His first miracle. A wedding feast had run out of wine. He instructed the servants to fill the water pots with water. Jesus proceeded to transfer the water into the most delectable wine that the Governor of the feast had ever tasted!

Keep in mind that until modern times; there was no running water, and no sewer systems. There wasn't even a drain in the sink! Pots, pans, bowls and buckets were more valuable than we can imagine.

"But in a great house there are not only vessels of gold and of silver, but also of wood and of earth; and some to honour, and some to dishonour" (II Timothy 2:20).

Each vessel in the home had a purpose and it was considered either clean, (a vessel of honor) or dirty (a vessel of dishonor). Vessels of honor were constantly filled, drawn from, cleansed and refilled. Vessels of dishonor held unclean things. Nothing was ever drawn from it because it was repugnant. It was a reproach and a disgrace to use water from a vessel of dishonor.

In scripture, we are referred to as vessels. "If a man therefore purge himself from these, he shall be a vessel unto honour, sanctified, and meet for the master's use, and prepared unto every good work" (II Timothy 2:21). In other words, we are vessels of God and God wants us to be vessels of honor.

When pottery is found in an archeological dig, Archeologists ask two major questions: What is it made of? What was its purpose? Today, Jesus asks the same two questions of us: "What are we made of?" and "What is our purpose?" (in other-words, "What are we filled with?")

"He that believeth on me, as the scripture hath said, out of his belly shall flow rivers of living water. (But this spake he of the Spirit, which they that believe on him should receive: for the Holy Ghost was not yet given; because that Jesus was not yet glorified)" (John 7:38, 39).

How about your vessel? Have you been filled with the Holy Ghost?

One of the Lord's biggest frustrations when He was on earth, was the religious order of the day—the Pharisees and Saducees were not vessels of honor, they were vessels of dishonor. Jesus called them "whited seplecures." He told them they were full of dead men's bones. He went on to explain that they were clean on the outside but filthy on the inside. Because they weren't honoring God in what they were doing or how they were living, they were vessels of dishonor.

As His creation, Jesus desires us to be vessels of honor. He wants us to be overflowing with His Spirit. He wants us to be drawn from daily as we share our lives with others. He wants us to be cleansed and refilled every day. He *doesn't* want us to become stagnate.

If a container sits too long, the contents spoil. The spoiled food must be emptied, and the container must be scrubbed and disinfected so that it might be used again. If our heart becomes stagnate, filled with unclean thoughts and feelings, we need to do the same thing! Our heart needs to be emptied. Then it needs to be scrubbed and disinfected by the Word of God so that it might be used again.

The Bible tells us that we are washed by the "watering of the word". We are cleansed as we read His Word, as we pray and as we hear the preaching of the Word. Some messages we hear at church are just like scouring powder! They get down on the inside and clean out all of the junk that has attached itself to us! The purpose of the preached word is to cleanse our mind, our heart, and our soul.

After we are cleansed, we need to guard our heart so unclean things don't have a chance to grow inside our vessel again.

Think back to the beginning of this chapter. What type of vessel did you say you would like to be? Did you choose something practical like a mixing bowl, or something beautiful like a vase or fancy teacup? Always keep in mind that it doesn't matter to God if we are not the most beautiful vessel physically. Scripture says that man looks on the outward appearance, but God looks on the heart. What matters to God is what's on the inside: what we are really made of and what our purpose is!

In Paul's day, clay pottery was very common. It was plentiful and it was cheap, much like our Styrofoam cups are today. In II Corinthians, Paul talks about the *ministry*, the *glorious gospel* of Jesus Christ and about the *good news*.

"For God, who commanded the light to shine out of darkness, hath shined in our hearts, to give the light of the knowledge of the glory of God in the face of Jesus Christ. But we have this treasure in earthen vessels, that the excellency of the power may be of God, and not of us" (II Corinthians 4:6,7).

If Paul were preaching to us to day, he would probably say, "We have *this treasure, this light, this glorious gospel, in Styrofoam cups!*" He was saying that *what the vessel is made of, is not nearly as important as what is in the vessel!*

Now I ask you the question: What is in your vessel?

I don't know if you've noticed, but God has a tremendous sense of humor. I love the story I mentioned earlier, of Jesus' first miracle at the wedding feast.

"And there were set there six waterpots of stone, after the manner of the purifying of the Jews, containing two or three firkins apiece. Jesus saith unto them, Fill the waterpots with water. And they filled them up to the brim. And he saith unto them, Draw out now, and bear unto the governor of the feast.

And they bare it. When the ruler of the feast had tasted the water that was made wine, and knew not whence it was: (but the servants which drew the water knew;) the governor of the feast called the bridegroom, And saith unto him, Every man at the beginning doth set forth good wine; and when men have well drunk, then that which is worse: but thou hast kept the good wine until now" (John 2: 6-10).

I don't know if you caught the significance of the vessels Jesus had the servants get. They were vessels used for purifying for ceremonial cleansing, the vessels used for washing their feet! Jesus used unclean vessels to work His miracle! The ruler didn't know where the vessels came from, but the servants did!

Now I ask you, what was your vessel like before Jesus got hold of it? Mine was unclean. It was a vessel of dishonor! But Jesus worked a miracle in my vessel! He made me fit for the Master's use, a vessel He can dwell in. He made me a vessel of honor!

Have *you* given Jesus your vessel? God has a purpose for every vessel that is made available to Him. He desires to use you to do a work for Him. He desires to let His glorious light shine through you as you live for Him.

Let me close with this little story:

A water bearer in India had two large pots; each hung on the end of a pole, which he carried across his neck. One of the pots had a crack in it and while the other pot was perfect and always delivered a full portion of water at the end of the long walk from the stream to the master's house, the cracked pot arrived only half full. For a full two years this went on daily, with the bearer delivering only one and a half pots full of water in his master's house. Of course, the perfect pot was proud of its accomplishments, perfect to the end for which it was made. But the poor cracked pot was ashamed of its own imperfection, and miserable that it was able to accomplish only half of what it had been made to do.

After two years of what it perceived to be a bitter failure, it spoke to the water bearer one day by the stream. "I am ashamed of myself, and I want to apologize to you." "Why?" asked the bearer. "What are you ashamed of?" "I have been able, for these past two years, to deliver only half my load because this crack in my side causes water to leak out all the way back to your master's house. Because of my flaws, you have to do all this work, and you don't get full value from your efforts," the cracked pot said.

The water bearer felt sorry for the old cracked pot, and in his compassion he said, "As we return to the master's house, I want you to notice the beautiful flowers along the path." Indeed, as they went up the hill, the old cracked pot took notice of the sun warming the beautiful wild flowers on the side of the path, and this cheered it some. But at the end of the trail, it still felt bad because it had leaked out half its load, and so again it apologized to the bearer for its failure.

The bearer said to the pot, "Did you notice that there were flowers only on your side of the path, but not on the other pot's side? That's because I have always known about your flaw, and I took advantage of it. I planted flower seeds on your side of the path, and every day while we walk back from the stream, you've watered them. For two years I have been able to pick these beautiful flowers to decorate my master's table. Without you being just the way you are, he would not have this beauty to grace his house."

Each of us has our own unique flaws. We are all cracked pots to some degree, but if we will allow it, the Lord will use our flaws to grace His table. In God's economy, nothing that is made available to Him will go to waste!

Give yourself to God completely. Serve Him in Spirit and truth and you too can be a vessel of honor!

Chapter Two
Our Search For Significance

"Who am I? And what am I doing here?" We've all thought this at some point in our life, but few of us would ever voice it at a nationally televised presidential debate as Admiral James Stockdale did when he ran for Vice President with Ross Perot.

"Who am I?" is an ageless question. Adolescents struggle with it for years. If left unanswered, it continues to haunt them into adulthood. Unfortunately, some people never find out who they are.

People, who don't really know who they are, struggle with debilitating low self-esteem. Because they never seem to meet their own expectations, they're sure they don't meet the "perceived" expectations of others. They consider themselves failures and live life far below God's promise of abundant life. One person accurately said, "I am who *I think you think I am.*"

"You shall know the truth and the truth shall make you free..." (John 8:32) is not just talking about freedom in salvation but rather freedom in every area of our lives: our goals, our motives, and our sense of self worth. Today, we give lip service to *spiritual truths*, but we don't really allow them to affect us in a tangible way, especially in the area of self-esteem.

Instead of looking to God to meet our needs, we continue to look to the world for our security and purpose. We seek personal success, status, beauty, wealth, and the approval of others. We drive ourselves to achieve, doing anything to make others happy or to impress them. We spend countless hours and dollars to look and smell appropriately. We avoid situations and people where the risks of failure and rejection are high. As a result of this, we find it difficult to witness to others about the love of Christ and His ability to make us a new creature in Him.

We all know that life is a "rat race," but we fail to realize that we can't win by running faster. We need to learn how to apply God's truth to help us live for Christ rather than for the approval of other people.

We have all experienced hurts in our lives that affect the way we relate to people and respond to situations. We develop defense mechanisms to block the pain and gain significance. We try to hide our loneliness, hurt and anger because "good Christians" don't experience those feelings. We all want to be "good Christians" so we're not really honest with ourselves, with God, or with anyone else.

God wants us to be honest with Him. David said, "Surely you desire truth in the inner parts; you teach me wisdom in the inmost place" (Psalms 51:6 NIV).

David was honest with God. He told God when he felt despair, when he was confused, and when he was angry with others. He admitted his sin to God. He told God he loved him and trusted in Him. He gave God praise. David did not lead a perfect life before God, but he was willing and open in all areas to be seen by God. He did not allow the praise of men to give him the significance that he knew came only from God. When David was anointed King, there weren't many men that even knew it. He had to trust in the knowledge that the calling had come from God Himself and realize that without the hand of God, he was nothing.

In our own lives, the desire for acceptance pressures us to perform for the praise of others. We must come to the point in life where we realize that lasting peace will never come when we continually have to prove ourselves to others, but rather when we are accountable to God. Our soul's significance comes only from our creator.

Sometimes in our relationships we look to a person, it could be our spouse, a child, or a friend, to always be loving, accepting and forgiving. We become frustrated when they can't meet these needs. This leads some to commit adultery in an attempt to have their perceived needs met. What we fail to realize is that these are attributes that can only be fulfilled by God. Our true significance and worth is only found in Him.

Genesis 1 & 2 tells of the creation of man. Man was made in the image and likeness of God. He was created to govern the earth and have fellowship with God. God put man in an environment that met every one of his needs. If you have children, think for a moment about the birth of your first child. How did you feel? You wanted to meet every one of that child's needs. Every whimper found you by the bedside trying to comfort or provide a need. That is what God is trying to do for us today, but all too often we choose to have our needs met by someone else or something else.

John 10:10 tells us that God wants us to experience abundant life! That doesn't mean that God will remove all obstacles from our life, but that He will help us to apply His solutions to the problems we face along the way.

We must have an accurate perception of ourselves, of God and of others, based on the truths of God's word. Robert McGee, professional counselor and author, says, "An accurate, biblical self-concept contains both strength and humility, both sorrow over sin and joy about forgiveness, a deep sense of our need for God's grace and a deep sense of the reality of God's grace."

An accurate understanding of self-esteem or self worth is crucial to our emotional, spiritual, and social stability and is the driving element within the human spirit. We all have the need for positive self-esteem; our problem is that we look to others for our significance rather than God. People will fail us. Our own parents may have "failed" us, but God will **never** fail us! He created us and only He has the capacity or ability to fulfill all of our needs to make us a ***significant*** person.

In the beginning, God created Adam and Eve secure and free. Nothing compared to them. They were created complete and perfect in the image of God. Their purpose was to reflect the image and glory of God. They were to be the showcase of God's creation. They were *significant*! Then sin entered the picture. McGee says, "One of the tragic implications of this event is that man lost his *secure* status with God and began to struggle with feelings of arrogance, inadequacy, and despair, *valuing the opinions of others* more than the truth of God. This has robbed man of his true self-worth and has put him on a continual, but fruitless search for significance through his success and the approval of others."

In other words, Satan robbed man of his true self-worth. Satan robbed man of his true purpose—of his significance in God. Separated from God and His word, people have only their abilities and the opinions of others on which to base their worth. They allow the circumstances around them to ultimately control the way they feel about themselves. One of Satan's ultimate lies is *Self-Worth = Performance + Others' Opinions*.

God desires that we be restored to the destiny He created us for. We are new creatures in Christ but we need to grow in the understanding of where our significance truly is: *Our Significance (Our Self-Worth) = Christ*.

It doesn't matter what people think of us. We simply need to look to God! Our earthly significance is in *Him* alone. *In God, we are somebody!*

Chapter Three

He Didn't Lift Us Up To Let Us Down!

The more I read the Bible, the more I realize that over the past 6,000 years, mankind really hasn't changed much! There are times when we feel great faith, we're on the mountaintop, and everything's going great! Then there are times when we feel like we have no faith, we're in the deepest valley and nothing's going right!

Sometimes those "highs" and "lows" are moments apart! And at the most, they're only days apart!

We have faith; we want to have faith. We believe in God. We know He knows what's best for us, but we allow our emotions to get in our way. We allow our carnal nature to void our spiritual desires and destroy our faith.

Again, we really haven't changed much this last 6,000 years!

The Children of Israel had toiled under Pharaoh's hand in the land of Egypt for four hundred years. They had prayed for deliverance for centuries. They had pleaded with God and believed that some day a deliverer would come. Finally, Moses came on the scene. At first they followed his leading, obeyed his commands and eventually did leave Egypt. Then what happened? As soon as they got out of town, just three short days later, they started their next round of complaining! Moses wasn't leading them right, God wasn't feeding them right, they couldn't overcome their enemies... So a fourteen-day trip took them forty years and most of them never saw God's total plan for their deliverance!

II Kings tells the story of the prophets Elisha and Elijah. Elisha, a young prophet, followed Elijah as closely as he could, because Elijah had promised him a double portion of his spirit if he was there and saw him when he ascended into heaven. The text reads:

"And Elisha saw it, and he cried, My father, my father, the chariot of Israel, and the horsemen thereof. And he saw him no more: and he took hold of his own clothes, and rent them in two pieces. He took up also the mantle of Elijah that fell from him, and went back, and stood by the bank of Jordan; And he took the mantle of Elijah that fell from him, and smote the waters, and said, Where is the LORD God of Elijah? and when he also had smitten the waters, they parted hither and thither: and Elisha went over. And when the sons of the prophets which were to view at Jericho saw him, they said, The spirit of Elijah doth rest on Elisha. And they came to meet him, and bowed themselves to the ground before him. And they said unto him, Behold now, there be with thy servants fifty strong men; let them go, we pray thee, and seek thy master: lest peradventure the spirit of the LORD hath taken him up, and cast him upon some mountain, or into some valley. And he said, Ye shall not send. And when they urged him till he was ashamed, he said, Send. They sent therefore fifty men; and they sought three days, but found him not. And when they came again to him, (for he tarried at Jericho,) he said unto them, Did I not say unto you, Go not?" (II Kings 2:12).

Can you imagine that? The sons of the prophets were the Bible College of the day. They actually thought God had dropped Elijah upon some mountain and left him there!

Elisha tried to tell them that he knew God had not dropped Elijah from his chariot and left him to die in the wilderness. He tried to tell them that God didn't lift him up to let him down! But the prophets insisted and pushed Elisha until they made him feel ashamed and embarrassed, so he sent some of them to check it out.

Then there was Peter. Peter saw Jesus walking on the water and begged to join Him. He had all the faith he needed when he stepped out of the boat. But then he looked down. He saw that what he was doing was not humanly possible, even though he *was* doing it! At that moment, he took his eyes off Jesus. He looked at his circumstances and *knew* that what he was doing couldn't be done! All of a sudden, his faith left him! When his faith left him, his emotions took control. God didn't lift him up to let him down! Peter let himself down, and he let the Lord down when he doubted that what he was doing was real!

Unfortunately, time and again, I have been guilty of the same thing in my own life. I'll never forget the year I was pregnant with our second child. As a couple, we had discussed having another baby and I was *sure* I would be able to continue to teach school after the baby was born. The babysitter situation was settled. Everything seemed to be great. Then it hit!

All of a sudden our plans collapsed. Our babysitter called to say that she couldn't baby-sit anymore and I began to realize that I *really* didn't want to work anymore. I wanted to stay home with my little ones, but at that point, it was too late! We quickly made other arrangements, and I went back to work.

That entire year, I prayed that the Lord would make a way for me to stay at home. Two years earlier we had bought a house that took both of our incomes, so it really seemed out of the question. Fitting two salaries into one didn't work on paper and my husband was a little upset with me for having changed my mind about working!

After a year of much prayer, tears and frustration, the Lord opened up an unbelievable door for us. Not only did He make a way for me to stay at home with the children, He also opened a full-time ministry position for my husband.

We put our house up for sale and moved to Indianapolis, where my husband became the Principal of Calvary Christian School. He went to work every day and I stayed at home with our two children in the evangelist's quarters. I should have been thanking God for allowing me to be home with our children, but it didn't take long before I was just as frustrated as before, but for a different reason. After all, my husband was leading an exciting life! He was meeting people I had only heard of! All sorts of exciting things were happening at the school and church and he was a part of it! There I was, stuck at home with two little ones and very little money, while he was going out to lunch and talking with all of those interesting people....

I had become just like the children of Israel and Peter! I had prayed and pleaded with God to make a way for me to stay home with my children. When it came to pass, I wasn't satisfied and began to grumble and complain, feeling somehow that the Lord had let me down. I was just like the Israelites who took their eyes off God and looked at their circumstances. I had allowed my emotions to destroy all God had graciously done for me.

It took about two weeks for me to wake up to what was happening. When I did, you can imagine how I felt. I felt like a heel! I asked God to forgive me for grumbling and complaining. Once again, He forgave me, as He so generously does; and I went on to have three of the richest and most fulfilling years of my life as I watched our little ones grow!

As human beings we are extremely vulnerable to the attack of the enemy when we take our eyes off Jesus and look at our circumstances. **Satan uses our emotions to override our reason. When we allow our emotions to control us, we begin a roller coaster ride of highs and lows.** Satan looks for every opportunity to destroy us. He would like for us to be controlled by emotions rather than reason. His purpose is to kill, steal and destroy all that we have, all that we are and all that we ever hope to be.

Satan tries to get us "coming and going," as the old saying goes. He gets us riled up and upset about situations and when the situation is resolved in our heart and life, he comes at us from another angle, telling us that we have no hope and that we have blasphemed God. Remember: Satan is the author of confusion. God *is not* the author of confusion. We must allow God to help us to see through the devil's devices. When our guard is down, Satan uses our emotions to defeat us.

Emotions are powerful forces in the human mind, but we cannot stand on them! They are fickle, unreliable and sometimes extremely foolish! We must stand on the never changing rock—Christ Jesus!

Modern Psychology and "the world" say, "If it *feels* good, do it!" They encourage us to allow our emotions to overrule reason. God intended *His reason* to overrule our emotions. Our emotions must always be accountable to the power of reason and will. We can "will" or "set" our mind to do impossible things—when God controls us through our reason and not our feelings. We need to "set our face" toward the Lord. "I have set the LORD always before me: because he is at my right hand, I shall not be moved" (Psalms 16:8). (I shall not be moved, means I will not allow my emotions to control me.)

Emotions, like roller coasters, fluctuate up and down, from highs to lows. Stability comes from our determination to serve God, regardless of the circumstances. To do right, regardless of how we "feel."

Satan doesn't give up on us just because we are committed Christians. He tries one tactic after another. He stealthily uses weapons of guilt, rejection, fear, embarrassment, grief, depression, loneliness and misunderstandings to destroy our stability, and to make us distrust God's ability to meet our needs.

When we rely on our emotions, we open the door to the devil's devices. Always remember: his entire goal is to destroy us.

Take fear for example, it has a remarkable way of generating evidence to support itself. You hear a strange noise and it doesn't take long for an entire scenario to appear in your mind and with the direst of consequences! Dr James Dobson related a story about his parents in the 1960's. One night his mother thought she heard someone in the house and she convinced herself that it was Charles Manson and his murderous followers who just happened to be locked up in prison!

Then there is guilt. The devil prods you to commit sin and if you fall into the trap, realize it and repent, he's right there to tell you that it's too late. He tells you that you have blasphemed the Holy Ghost, and you can't ever be forgiven, so you might as well just continue to sin.

He also uses rejection. He tells you that no one loves you so how could God possibly love you? People who have felt rejection from their family, their father in particular, are vulnerable to this attack. Subconsciously, we often relate to God as we do to our earthly father. If your father was not loving and kind, it may be hard for you to relate to God as being loving and kind.

Loneliness goes hand in hand with rejection. When people are lonely, the devil tells them all sorts of things and opens up opportunities to sin. People who feel lonely or rejected by their spouse, often fall into sexual sins.

A person once told me that they felt that they should leave their church because they were so lonely. They didn't have any friends in the church. They thought that if they went to a larger church they would have friends. I asked the person if they had friends in the last church they were in and they said no. They also told me that no one in their family liked them either. Believe me, changing churches isn't going to help that person. They will take their loneliness with them and still not feel like they have any friends! They must allow God to help them get out of Satan's trap.

Then there are misunderstandings. If you have ever played "telephone," you know how easy it is to mistake what someone has said. When information passes through two or three people, it seldom resembles the original message!

We need to face the fact that we are all going to have experiences or opportunities where we think God has let us down. We must be spiritually strong enough that we do not allow our emotions to get in the way of what we know is right!

Many Godly people have felt as you have

God told Noah to build a boat on dry land and to preach righteousness. It took him one hundred years to do so, but he did, and his family was saved. During that time, as he was prodded and mocked, I am sure that he had lonely times.

Abraham was told he would have a son and that he would have as many descendants as there were grains of sand on the earth—but Abraham didn't wait on God. Perhaps he thought God had let him down. He accepted a man-made substitute and the world is still paying for it today.

Jonah was told to warn a nation so they could repent and be saved—but he ran from God. When he finally obeyed God and warned the people, he was angry with God because the people did repent and God didn't destroy them! God forgave the people, but Jonah couldn't!

Job lost all he had—but he didn't "curse God and die" as his wife advised him to do. He "maintained his integrity with God."

John the Baptist ended up in prison as a result of preaching righteousness and the coming of Jesus. The devil tortured him to the point that he sent word to Jesus, "Are you the Christ or do we look for another?"

So the sons of the prophets were not alone in thinking God might have let them down. The truth of the matter is that God doesn't let us down. We let ourselves down by:
- Unrealistic expectations of life, ourselves and others
- Lack of commitment to God and family
- Lack of restraint (self-control)
- Impatience, unwillingness to wait
- Unbalanced commitment to work, church, etc., resulting in extreme fatigue
- Reaching for the unobtainable things of the past
- Unrighteous anger, envy and jealousy

Do you realize that as Christians we are more likely to sin by our reactions to situations than by our original actions? We are not nearly as likely to go to the local bar for a beer as we are to envy someone's new house or get angry because our husband tracked mud on the floor we just scrubbed!

At some point in our walk with God, we must learn to control our emotions. Controlling our emotions is a matter of spiritual maturity. Spiritual maturity is *not* blaming God when things don't go just as we thought they would. It is *not* jumping to conclusions before we have all the facts. Spiritual maturity *is* setting our mind and our will to keep our eyes on Jesus, regardless of the way circumstances appear. It *is* obedience to God in times of crises. It is self-control. It is commitment to God and commitment to family.

Today we have so many things we can place our trust in: husband, job, education, finances, Social Security, the government... but these things will all let us down! The things of this world are all temporal. But we serve a God that changes not! A God that lifts us up and never lets us down! Study His word, memorize it and be ready when the fiery darts of the enemy try to come against you.

"Above all, taking the shield of faith, wherewith ye shall be able to quench all the fiery darts of the wicked" (Ephesians 6:16).

"The LORD redeemeth the soul of his servants: and none of them that trust in him shall be desolate" (Psalms 24:22).

"Trust in the LORD with all thine heart; and lean not unto thine own understanding" (Proverbs 3:5).

"O Lord by God, in thee do I put my trust: save me from all them that persecute me, and deliver me" (Psalms 7:1).

"Some [trust] in chariots, and some in horses: but we will remember the name of the Lord our God" (Psalms 20:7).

"Therefore, my beloved brethren, be ye stedfast, unmoveable, always abounding in the work of the Lord, for as much as ye know that your labour is not in vain in the Lord" (I Corinthians 15:58).

"Stand fast therefore in the liberty wherewith Christ hath made us free, and be not entangled again with the yoke of bondage" (Galations 5:1).

We cannot allow our emotions, or feelings, to get in the way of doing what we know is right. Giving in to our emotions and allowing them to be our guiding factor, makes us double minded. When we are ruled by our emotions, we are vulnerable to every ungodly thing. "A doubleminded man is unstable in all his ways" (James 1:8).

We *are* going to have difficult times. Scripture says that the rain falls on the just and on the unjust. Jesus said that we will be hated among all men for His namesake. We will have persecution, but regardless of what we go through, we have got to trust in God. We have got to "set our face" to serve the Lord.

If you don't *know* God in this power, you *can* know Him. You can be filled with His Spirit. The Book of Acts tells us that Jesus desires to fill us with His Spirit, which is the power to overcome the will and desires of the flesh.

On the day of Pentecost, the first day of the church, Peter took the "keys to the kingdom" (Matthew 16:19) that Jesus gave him. In Acts 2:38, Peter used the keys to open up the kingdom of heaven through salvation: Repentance, baptism in Jesus name and receiving the gift of the Holy Ghost. Jesus said that He had to go away, but that He would not leave us comfortless. He said that the Holy Ghost, or Holy Spirit, would be our comforter. Truly the Holy Spirit is our comforter even today as we seek to control our emotions rather than allow them to control us.

Never loose sight of the fact that Jesus didn't lift us up to let us down! He lifted us up to live with Him in all eternity! In all things, trust Him!

Chapter Four

The Ugly Duckling

The Ugly Duckling is a famous fairy tale written by Hans Christian Anderson. He tells the story of a mother duck that patiently waited for her eggs to hatch. Finally, one by one the eggs began to crack. From each shell came a tiny golden creature crying, "Peep! Peep!" Soon all the eggs were hatched, except one, the largest one.

At last the final egg hatched. A young bird peeked out, crying "Peep! Peep!" like the others. But this duckling was gray and quite large, and very ugly.

The Mother Duck stared at her new baby and wondered if it was really a turkey and not a duckling at all! She took her ducklings to the riverbank to practice their swimming. Mother Duck watched her largest baby, because she knew that turkeys couldn't swim.

All the ducklings jumped fearlessly into the river, even the ugly duckling swam gracefully. "That settles it," thought Mother Duck, "he is not a turkey after all!"

Mother Duck took the ugly duckling with the rest of her family, to live on a farm but all of the other ducks picked on the ugly duckling, calling him names and stealing his food. Even the chickens laughed at him and a turkey pecked at him viciously.

The poor ducking decided he must run away. "There is no home for an ugly duckling," he said miserably and sadly waddled away.

Through the winter, he almost starved and nearly froze. Then one day spring came. The duckling tested his wings and found that they were strong and that he was able to fly. He flew, landing by chance in a beautiful garden with a very clear pond. Swimming there, were three beautiful white swans.

The duckling swam toward the beautiful swans, though he knew they would laugh and tell him to go away. "I'd just like to see them, if only for a moment," thought the ugly duckling.

But the swans did not laugh or tell him to go away. The swans stroked his neck and welcomed him. The duckling happened to glance down at the water, where he saw his own reflection. Wonder of wonders! He was no longer a gray, ugly bird. He had grown up to be a beautiful white swan!

In Europe, where this story originated, swans are the birds of royalty. The little duckling was a symbol of the royal family and did not even know it.

We are often like that little swan. We do not realize whose child we really are! We forget whose family we belong to! We go through life seeing ourselves as we *think* others see us and we develop a negative self-image.

We become unhappy with who we are: we're too tall, we're too short, too fat or too thin. We're awkward and clumsy, our hair is the wrong color and we can't do a thing with it! The list goes on and on.

Just as the little duck, we feel isolated, misunderstood and unloved. Because we do not "feel" loved or lovely, we put ourselves down to the point that we are unable to accept a compliment.

How many times have you received a compliment only to turn it away? A friend says, "What a pretty dress!" You respond with, "Oh I've had it for ages. It's just an old thing I drug out of the closet." Instead of politely saying, "Thank you, it's one of my favorites," or "Thank you, I made it myself."

At some point in our lives, we need to get to the same place as the young duck. He was drawn to the beauty of the swans and *boldly* joined them, risking the certainty of once again being turned away. However, when he joined them and chanced to look at his reflection in the pond, he found that he was just as beautiful as they were! "But we all, with open face beholding as in a glass the glory of the Lord, are changed into the same image from glory to glory, even as by the Spirit of the Lord" (II Corinthians 3:18).

In II Corinthians Chapter 3, Paul was trying to encourage the people to realize who they were in Christ. He was confident in who he was and wanted them to have the same understanding. Verses 1-18, as paraphrased from The New International Version, say: "Do we have to tell you again who we are in Christ? Or do we have to prove something to you? You are a living epistle, a letter written and known by all men! It's not of ourselves, our competence comes from God! We have a hope! We are bold! We reflect the Lord's glory!"

I have never been one who liked to look in mirrors. I have never felt I was "pretty." I grew up with a negative self-image. I used to tell people that I was born a size 12! But in 1980, God did something in my life that I will never forget. He let me know that He loves me for who I am. He is not concerned about the dress size I wear or my outward "beauty." He simply loves me the way I am! Scripture declares over and over that we are precious in the sight of God. I *finally* understood it!

"The LORD seeth not as man seeth; for man looketh on the outward appearance, but the LORD looketh on the heart" (I Samuel 16:7).

"We are a peculiar treasure" (Exodus 19:5).

"We are chosen by Jehovah" (Deuteronomy 14:2).

"We are the apple of His eye" (Deuteronomy 32:10).

"Thou shalt also be a crown of glory in the hand of the Lord, and a royal diadem in the hand of thy God" (Isaiah 62:3).

And they shall be mine in that day when I make up my jewels!" (Malachi 3:17).

What has God done for you? When you look in the mirror, do you see the same person you saw before you came to know God? We must realize that when we look in a mirror that we don't see ourselves as God sees us! He sees us as He has transformed us!

When we are open faced before God, we are changed into ***His*** glory by ***His*** spirit. It is the spirit of the Lord that does the changing! We need to accept this as a fact! We also need to make sure that we are glorifying God in all our actions. Putting ourselves down ***does not*** glorify God; it only detracts from His glory. I have heard it said that either we glorify God or we detract from His glory in everything we say and do.

God sees us with "crowns of glory." Corinthians tells us that a woman's uncut hair is "her glory." "But if a woman have long hair, it is a glory to her..." (I Corinthians 11:15).

Jesus sees what we have become in Him, what He has transformed us into. Imagine how Mary Magdalene felt when she realized that she was the first person to see Jesus after His resurrection! Her past was behind her. She had been forgiven of all her sins and was honored by God to be the first to see Him when He rose from the dead! I am sure her self esteem rose tremendously when she realized the gift God had given her, to be in His very presence!

Jesus said that we are a chosen generation, a royal Priesthood. We have been bought with a ***great price***: the ***very blood*** of the Lord Jesus Christ!

We must be the person God has made us. We cannot keep trying to be someone we're not, mistakenly thinking that people will more readily accept us. We must also help others to accept themselves as God has made them!

I've known young people who grew up with severe physical handicaps, but never felt they were any different than anyone else. Their families simply loved them, accepted them, and helped them to be all that God desired of them.

Helen Keller became deaf and blind as a result of an infantile illness; yet, she became a prolific speaker and writer. Reverend Allen Oggs, born with Spinal-bifida and not expected to live for 24 hours, is approaching retirement, having fathered four children, written several books, evangelized, pastored and been a favored speaker for Focus on the Family's radio broadcast.

"Favour is deceitful, and beauty is vain: but a woman that feareth *(reverences, honors and respects)* the LORD, she shall be praised" (Proverbs 31:30).

Just as that young duck saw his reflection in the lake, we must see our reflection in Jesus Christ!

God desires that we grow spiritually in Him. We all do things that are not pleasing to Him. It's these things that we need to change and to improve upon. When you study the personalities (in another chapter), you will have a clearer understanding of both your positive and negative traits. If you desire to grow in God, He will be happy to reveal the areas of spiritual growth that He feels you should improve upon!

Chapter Five
The Cinderella Syndrome

Do you remember the story of Cinderella? Long ago and faraway.... We all have a past, and just as Cinderella, some of us have had a miserable existence with many hurts, and severe disappointments. Many have been violated physically and emotionally, and like Cinderella, most of us have had a secret hope for the future: a hope and dream that someday everything will be better.

I remember telling my husband, "If you marry me, you'll really have to show me a lot of love." I was warning him what I felt I needed after we were married. I was warning him that I would require his undying affection and attention. I was warning him that he had a big job ahead!

Just as Cinderella, I believed that once I was married, my problems would be over. Prince Charming would sweep me off my feet and we would live happily ever after! I had it all planned out, we would marry, have children and teach school. Everything would be perfect.

Most women are the same, when we met the man of our dreams, no one could tell us that he wasn't "Mr. Right." Regardless of what others might have seen in him, we only saw the best. We saw no flaws, and had no misgivings. No amount of talking could convince us otherwise. We were sure that it was God's will for us to marry him, no questions asked and nothing to discuss!

Then we marry, only to find out that the very person we were depending on for our happiness, provision and protection, isn't perfect! He doesn't think at all like we do. He doesn't like everything we cook. He doesn't help around the house. He leaves the cap off the toothpaste and his socks on the floor. Either he's too particular or he's a slob! He's a tightwad or he spends too much money. We find out that he doesn't even like to go shopping anymore! You know the story!

Then we start to wonder, "Is this the same man I dated for so long? I thought that surely I knew him by now. Was this really God's will?"

Then we decide, if this is how he really is, surely God has had me marry him so that I can change him! We begin to pressure him to conform to our standards, but things usually get worse. Our fairy tale life soon collapses as we become disappointed, disenchanted and disillusioned.

Because things haven't worked out as we thought they would, we begin the "If Only" routine. We look back, into our past, thinking: "If only I hadn't married him, I never really loved him. My childhood wasn't so bad. I should never have turned down so-and-so. Yes, that must be it, I should have married him. Things would be different if...."

When you allow yourself to look into the past, you allow daydreams to set in that breed dissatisfaction. Some women look for an escape, so they read steamy romantic novels or watch soap operas that bring high expectations and unrealistic fantasies into their lives.

Even though we weren't happy before we were married, "The Cinderella Syndrome" convinces us that happiness was yesterday and will be again someday, but it definitely isn't now. Just as Jesus was crucified between two thieves, we crucify ourselves between two thieves: past and present. We become bound by a fairy tale mentality that robs us from living and enjoying today.

Fairy tales with "happy endings" offer unreal answers to difficult problems. Dependency on God is replaced by an imaginary fairy godmother or godfather with magic dust in their pocket. The Cinderella Syndrome frustrates it's victims. Under it's spell, people are bound by "if onlys" of the past and the "some days" of the future. "Hope deferred makes the heart sick" (Proverbs 13:12). This speaks of depression, and where there is never contentment.

Are you experiencing the Cinderella Syndrome in your own life?

Don't feel like you are the only one, even Mary and Martha fell into the trap of disillusioned thinking. John 11: 20-26 tells the story. Lazarus, their brother, was very sick. They had called for Jesus, but He didn't come in time to heal Lazarus. When He did arrive, their reaction was, "Lord, if only you had been here, our brother would not have died." and, "Yes, we know that he will rise in the resurrection of the dead." They believed that Jesus could have healed him had He come when Lazarus was still alive. They also believed that Lazarus would live in the future, but they couldn't comprehend any change in the present.

Jesus wanted them to believe for the present. You can hear His frustration as He responded with, " I am the resurrection, and the life: he that believeth in me, though he were dead, yet shall he live: And whosoever liveth and believeth in me shall never die. Believest thou this?" It was here that "Jesus wept." Many think Jesus was weeping over the death of His friend. I personally believe that Jesus wept, not because Lazarus had died, but because His followers, those He dearly loved, did not understand who He really was and what power He possessed.

Mary and Martha were not content with the fact that Jesus arrived when He did. They looked to the past and to the future, but failed to look to the present.

Everyone lives in a tent: Content or Discontent!

It is important that we come to a point in life where we are content, regardless of what state we are in. We can learn to be content in the present. Paul said, "I have learned to be content no matter what state I'm in," (Philippians 4:11). I Timothy 6:6 tells us that "Godliness with contentment is great gain."

With the amount of moving we have done as a result of being in the ministry, I've learned to take Paul's statement literally and figuratively! Whether you have money or you don't, whether you live in Ohio, California, Europe or

Wisconsin, God wants you to be content wherever you are, both spiritually and physically.

There are three basic enemies of contentment: the disillusioning past, the disappointing present and the disenchanting future.

The disillusioning past is filled with sinful personal failures, regrets, bitterness and thoughts of "The Good Old Days." We must believe and trust in the scripture that says, "But this one thing I do, forgetting those things which are behind, and reaching forth unto those things which are before..." (Philippians 3:13).

The disappointing present may involve a husband who doesn't make you happy, a job that doesn't challenge you, children that cause problems and conflict, financial struggles, envy of others who seem to have it all, and generally feeling unhappy and sorry for yourself.

The disenchanting future—just when things look like they'll get better, something happens to destroy the hope. You interview for a job, only to find that they gave it to someone else. You find the perfect apartment, but someone has already put a deposit on it.

To really change, to break out of the Cinderella Syndrome, the cycle must be broken. To break out of the cycle, you must first ask yourself two questions:
1. What do I really want?
2. How does what **I** want, line up with what God wants for me?

In reality, only God can provide what we need to make us happy, but seldom do we seek His help, or accept it when He offers. Unlike Cinderella, there is no fairy godmother in our life. Only Jesus can fulfill the longing of our heart and He demands that we have no other gods before Him; not children, husband, job, friends, material goods or good looks.

If we call ourselves a disciple of Jesus and continue to desire and seek after things that are not God's will (someone else's husband, a bigger and better house, or a car to show off) we are destined to live in frustration and discontent. If we set out to have our own way no matter what, we will become idolaters and God will let us have our way just as He did with the children of Israel. They wanted a king; however, God wanted to be their king. God tried to warn them of the consequences of having a king, but they demanded to be like everyone else. Colossians 3:5 tells us that covetousness = idolatry. In other words: when all of our strength becomes focused on fulfilling our dreams or fantasies, God is relegated to the shadows of our new idol.

Psalms 37:4 says that God will give us the desire of our heart. *Our* impatience demands to know "when?" When God answers with "Yes," "No," or "Wait," we are often not happy with His answer. The bottom line is that we are disappointed when He doesn't answer like *we think* He should and *as soon* as we think He should.

Today there is an "epidemic" of Cinderellas among Christians and non-Christians alike, but as Christians, the tendency is to "spiritualize" the fairy tale. God has promised us the "desires of our heart," we think that means God will provide our every want! What our "heart" wants and what our "flesh" wants, are two different things, but we often confuse them. Our heart wants and desires the things of God, our flesh wants and desires the material things of the world.

Three Myths of the Cinderella Syndrome

Someday my Prince will come... when he comes, things may go well at first, but life soon becomes routine. Women fall into the trap of fantasy, expecting their husband to be the perfect romantic they see on the screen or read about, which no earthly man can fulfill daily. As one author said, "Husbands don't have scriptwriters." If you find yourself discontent before marriage, you will find you are discontent after you marry. Contentment has little to do with position (married or unmarried), it has everything to do with disposition!

Someday my people will change... In wanting our kids and husband to change to meet our standards, we wage war on them. Scripture never tells us we have to change others. We are the ones who are supposed to change as we grow in Christ. When I was a child, I spake as a child, I understood as a child, I thought as a child: but when I became a man, I put away childish things" (1 Corinthians 13:11). In other words, I grew up.

What we need to realize is that we don't have to feel like victims because others don't meet our desires or our expectations. We ***can*** find contentment in life in spite of those around us. I truly believe that ***happiness is a choice***. We make of life what we choose to, with the help of God.

Someday my prosperity will arrive...We'd all like to have the Midas Touch wouldn't we? We want a break financially, and then we're sure our life will be better. We don't believe in lotteries but the Publisher's Clearing House is fair game—so we buy magazine subscriptions in hope of winning the big one, right? We have all heard of depressed, reclusive, unhappy millionaires, so what makes us think we'll be any different?

Again, the truth is that only God can satisfy the longings of our heart, but ***we*** must be willing to ***allow*** Him to do so! We must believe that the past is under the blood and that "all things work to the good" as Jesus promised in Romans 8:28.

Start With The Past

To break the cycle, we have to start with the past—Once Upon A Time.... We need to face our own faults and not hold grudges. Some people torture themselves with the mistakes of the past in "shackles of regret." We must face facts—the past is over. Unfortunately it cannot be changed, but today and tomorrow ***can*** be changed.

People blame God for allowing things to happen to them, then take their frustrations out on their husband or their children because no one can really be mad at God, right? Most people want to blame their unhappiness on someone else: an unloving mother, a physically abusive father, a demanding teacher that embarrassed them, or a brother or sister.

Simply trying to bury the past doesn't help either. We don't have any science fiction time warp that it can get lost in. We have got to deal with it.

Confession, which is certainly underplayed today, really is a healing force. "Confess your faults one to another, and pray one for another, that ye may be healed. The effectual fervent prayer of a righteous man availeth much" (James 5:16).

We find ourselves not telling others what has happened to us, or what we've done for several reasons: we feel that it's not anyone's business, it hurts to bring it up, or we are too proud or embarrassed by the mistakes we've made. Meanwhile, *the past* destroys *today* and the *future*. When we don't deal with it, we're constantly reminded of it. We live and breathe our past hurts and failures because that is all we can think of. We become crippled by it. We dwell on it so much that we become *just like* the one who hurt us and in turn, inflict the same type of hurts on others that we feel have devastated us. It becomes an excuse to be the way we are.

Again, the cycle must be broken. With a conscious effort and God's help, we can be healed. We *can* break the cycle. The past may explain our current behavior but we should grow up from there. We should never try to excuse ourselves because of past memories. Scripture declares that we are new creatures, old things have passed away and *all things* have become new.

God expects every living thing to grow. He wants the dead things of the past trimmed out of our lives. God wants us to learn from our past, *not live* in our past.

Unfortunately, the old saying, "Time heals all wounds" is not necessarily true. More than "time" is needed. We need to consciously work on and desire to be healed of our past. We have all been violated in some way; by someone who has never asked our forgiveness, so how can we truly forgive them?

Until we consciously deal with something that is unresolved

in our lives, it will continually come back to haunt us. We need to remember; "They" (whoever hurt you) may be responsible for the hurt in your past; *you* are responsible for the present.

How To Deal With Unresolved Issues From The Past

Get forgiveness – "If we confess our sins, He is faithful and just to forgive us our sins and to cleanse us from all unrighteousness" (1 John 1:9). The Lord's prayer instructs us to pray, "And forgive us our tresspasses as we forgive those who tresspass against us." First we must ask God for forgiveness. We need to lay all our sins before the Lord and repent of them. When we do this, He is faithful and just to forgive us and forget them.

Next we need to *give* forgiveness. This is where it gets tough!

Release the blame you have accounted to God – God, who we understand knows all things, had to know what happened to hurt us. Why did he allow it to happen? Why didn't He interfere? Perhaps without really wanting to, we question God continually, "Why? Why? Why?"

As a result, many are angry with God, or secretly resentful because He didn't intervene in the situation that hurt them so deeply.

At this point I want you to stop and think. Ask yourself, "Am I angry or resentful to God?" This is a very difficult question to answer, after all, God is God and how can I be angry with Him? There were those in the Bible who became angry with God.

In I Samuel 1:12-18 we find Hannah pouring out her complaint and grief to God. She admitted to God that she was angry. After she heard from the man of God, her countenance was "no more sad."

We see Job's wife very angry with God, but she refused to talk with Him. She told her husband to curse God and die.

Joseph, in all he went through, never blamed God for his

situation and without their apologies, he freely forgave his brothers who sold him into slavery.

We must "consciously" release the blame we have placed on God. We must tell Him out loud, as Hannah did, that we won't hold anger and resentment toward Him any longer. To grow spiritually, we must honestly trust and accept His decision to permit pain to enter our lives.

When people ask me why there is so much pain and suffering in the world when God is supposed to be such a loving a kind God, the only answer I can give them is that it is a result of the sin of man. God allows mankind a free choice in all they do. He desires that they serve Him, but the ultimate choice is theirs. Unfortunately, sin is man's choice.

We try so hard to cover things in our lives that have hurt us, but just like a fishing bobber, the harder we push them down, the quicker they pop up someplace else!

We have all had hurtful things happen to us. I know that my life wasn't nearly as tragic as many have faced, but there were some situations that hurt deeply. I really thought I had done a pretty good job of hiding the hurts and actually thought that I had gotten over my past. I was asked to speak at a Ladies Seminar in Germany on the topic, "Walk a Mile in Their Shoes." I was to address the problems and hurt that children face.

As I studied and prepared for the lesson, I found myself walking through the things in my past that had hurt me. I prayed and I cried and I asked God to help me personally to get beyond the things in my past that I was still holding onto. I know God helped me as I trudged through that process, but the real release came when I spoke to the ladies, when I verbalized the pain and the forgiveness.

Then I was *truly* free! Satan couldn't hold me down any longer! He couldn't replay the past and make it hurt anymore!

When you consciously forgive God, the healing can begin. The memory isn't gone but the hurt is.

***Forgive yourself* --**

We've all made mistakes, bad decisions, and poor choices. You must consciously forgive yourself for the sins you willingly and knowingly committed.

If God is willing to forgive you when you ask forgiveness, who are you to not be as generous? Are you greater than God? Don't be like the servant whose huge debt the master forgave, but he couldn't forgive a fellow servant whose debt was minor in comparison. If you can accept God's free gift of forgiveness, you really have no choice but to forgive yourself. Again, you won't forget the memory, but when Satan tries to throw your past sins up to you. Rebuke him. Command him in Jesus name to get behind you, (Matthew 16:23) to get back to the past where he belongs.

Forgive Others –People often ask, "How can I forgive someone if they don't deserve forgiveness and if they've never asked for my forgiveness?"

You need to face the fact that some people will never admit that they hurt you. Some may not even know that they hurt you by things they said or did.

When Jesus hung on the cross, He looked down upon His murderers and said, "Father, forgive them for they know not what they do." He forgave those that crucified Him, in the midst of their actions and surely without their desire.

Some of you are probably thinking, "How can you tell me to forgive, you weren't the victim…"

Again, the Lord's Prayer tells us that we will be forgiven of our tresspasses, or sins, *as we forgive* those who tresspass against us.

We really have no choice. *If* we forgive others, we are forgiven. ***If we don't*** forgive, we aren't forgiven.

But how do we forgive if we are still so angry?
1. Decide to forgive.
2. Say out loud, "I forgive _____."
3. Pray for the person that has hurt you so deeply. You can't hate someone you earnestly pray for.

How do you know if you've really forgiven the guilty party?

You will no longer hate or dislike them. You will literally feel sorry for them because of the way they have chosen to live. If you still want to hurt them, if you can still want revenge, you haven't totally forgiven them.

Look over your past at unresolved hurts and remember:
- Forgive God for permitting the situation to happen
- Seek His forgiveness for any mistakes or tresspasses on your part
- Speak the names of those that have hurt you out loud and verbally forgive them
- You may want to tell them face to face that you forgive them or write them a letter, but this is entirely up to you.
- If they are no longer living, pretend they are sitting in a chair and tell them out loud that you forgive them. Rehearse the situation and then release it.

Total forgiveness in your life releases you from bondage. You are free to experience life as never before. You are free to love, free to hope and free to dream! You *can* live your life free of all regrets.

Forgiveness is like antibiotic medication, you have to fill the entire prescription and take all the pills. It won't work sitting on your shelf in a bottle!

Only *you* have the power to forgive. Even God will not force you to forgive. You can choose to live in despair, blaming God, yourself and everyone else and remain unhappy. Or you can choose to accept life as Hannah, Job and Joseph realizing that no matter what happened to them they would trust in God that "All things work together to the good to those that love God and are called according to His purpose" (Romans 8:28).

Look to Today

Now that we've finished the job of forgiveness, and we've taken care of the past, let's look to today. In our search for significance, we must deal with who we are today.

Most of us want to be special in some aspect of our life. We want to be "somebody."

I heard about one lady who had gone to New York City to "make it" in the theater but the only job she could get was modeling underclothes and she got fired from that! People told her that she needed to go back home but she was so determined to get her name on a marquee, that she used her life savings to have her name posted on a huge billboard across the street from the main train station. Her joy was driving around the square to see her name in print and knowing that everyone else who drove around the square could see it. She wanted to "be somebody" any way she could.

We may not go to such extremes, but we do everything in our power to become a significant person. We want to be a good wife, mother, secretary, nurse, teacher, Christian…. More often than not, we look to others to establish our self worth. As I mentioned earlier, self-image is not what others think of me.

I remember going through the Super Mom phase. I was the best mom, best housekeeper, best cook, most economical shopper, best seamstress… I was the best of the best, **until** I hit "burnout!" Then I became the biggest crab you've ever seen! I was tired all the time. I was frustrated. I felt I was the only one working. I was the only one who really cared… After all, I did *everything*! My husband *never* helped. He was *always* gone, doing the Lord's work of course! Why did I have to ask him to take out the garbage? He could see the overflowing trash can just as well as I could! (*Everything, never,* and *always* are pretty powerful words that we tend to use when we are upset about things and the way they seem to be going!)

I had the Cinderella Syndrome. I was trying to prove to myself and to the world that I was the "best", that I was significant because of all the things I was capable of doing, evidently thinking that I would look better in their eyes.

I know I'm not the only one who's experienced this. Martha had been the super hostess. She'd done everything just right and Mary had not been any help at all. All Mary did was sit around at Jesus' feet as he taught his disciples. Finally, Martha couldn't take anymore. She marched straight to the Master. She let Jesus know that she was doing **all** the work and that Mary **never** helped with anything. She let Jesus know that she was frustrated with her sister.

"Martha, Martha," He sighed, "Mary hath chosen the better part." He didn't mean that what Martha was doing was wrong, but that her priorities were in the wrong place.

I have to admit that I'm a lot like Martha at times, but I am working on it!

Please, if you remember nothing else in this chapter, remember we **cannot rely** on people, places or things to make us happy. We can't sit around thinking: if only my circumstances were different, if I only had more money, if only I was pretty, if only people didn't just like me for my looks, if I could just loose some weight, if I didn't have this physical problem, if I were just more spiritual, if I was more like so and so, if I could just have a bigger house, if I only had a smaller house, if I only had children, if I didn't have children... surely I would be happy. ***Circumstances and people can not satisfy our emotional needs.***

We have got to come to a place in our lives when we understand that we are only significant in our relationship to God, not in relationship to people or circumstances. "But let each one examine his own work, and then he will have rejoicing in himself alone, and not in another" (Galatians 6:4).

I was asked to speak at one of our Ladies retreats when we lived in Germany. After one of the sessions, a lady approached me and asked this question, "How can God use you when you're so fat?"

Can you imagine how I would have felt if I was having a problem with self-image at the time she said that to me? My significance wasn't in what she thought of me, but rather what God thought of me.

We take God's gifts so for granted that we don't appreciate them. We **need** to count our blessings daily. Unfortunately, we never fully appreciate anything until we loose it or think it will be lost. We need to realize that success is not in getting what you want, but rather in enjoying what you have. If you want to make a comparison that counts: don't compare yourself with a millionaire, compare yourself with those that live in third world countries. You will find yourself viewing life from a different perspective.

Our tendency is to blame other people for our present state of mind. Other people do not make us feel a certain way. We create our own feelings by choice and habit. I heard a story about a man who worked in a tall building. Everyday he rode the elevator up to his floor. Everyday another man got on the elevator at the same time. On their way to the top, the second man would spit on the first man. The first man never responded. He just took out his hankie and wiped it off. One day when this happened, another person was on the elevator and he asked the first man, "How can you let him get away with that?" The first man responded with, "It's his problem, not mine."

How would you have responded?

We *allow* people or situations to affect us by how we choose to react. We *allow* ourselves to feel certain ways. We need to understand that we choose how we feel. **God doesn't want us to be** thermometers, reflecting the temperature of others or our situation, He wants us to be ***thermostats***, controlling the setting, or temperature in our own lives. In that way we make our own comfort zone. When we make the decision, no matter what happens, I'm going to be cheerful. I'm not going to let so and so get under my skin. We don't have to *hope* for a good day, we *know* we will have a good day. We can choose to have a good day. People's moods may change but God's never does.

What happens when we become dependent on others for our happiness? We make unrealistic demands on them. We must remember, they are not God. They are not perfect. They cannot meet all of our needs.

Hannah would have destroyed Samuel and herself, if after she received the child she prayed for, she looked to him for the source of her joy. She could have wrapped her entire life around him, but because she gave her "treasure," her prized possession to God, she was free to go on with life, knowing that everything else would be okay.

When I told my fiancé that he would *really* have to show me love, I was placing an undue burden on him. Later, when I received the Baptism of the Holy Spirit, I realized that God had the real love I was looking for! It would have been impossible for my husband to have ever met those expectations of love.

Women, who become emotionally dependent on a man, stay in abusive relationships. They feel their need to be "loved" and feel that they find love in their man, even though they are being mistreated. As women, we need to be emotionally dependent on God. Only He can give us the emotional stability and tranquility we need. "Commit thy way unto the LORD; trust also in him; and he shall bring it to pass" (Psalms 37:5). "Thou wilt keep him in perfect peace, whose mind is stayed on thee: because he trusteth in thee" (Isaiah 26:3).

What eventually happens in some women, who have been in abusive situations, is that they end up hating men and resisting male authority. They don't respect their husband or their pastor and they have no fear of God. They become embittered people with no hope.

We need a Godly balance in our lives. We must understand that we can be free to enjoy other people without depending on them. We need to be content to *do our best*, not *be the best*. We need to avoid having an unhealthy craving for the applause of people when the only applause that really matters is the applause of heaven!

If we want to be free to enjoy the present, we've got to realize that we are not responsible for the actions of others and that we can't allow the actions of others to destroy us. We have an individual responsibility to God. "Every man shall give account of himself before God" (Romans 14:12).

Ezekiel 18:20 in the Living Bible, says, "The one who sins is the one who dies. The son shall not be punished for his father's sins, nor the father of his son's. The righteous person will be rewarded for his own goodness, and the wicked person for his own wickedness."

You are not responsible for the actions of others. You are not a failure because others chose wrongly. Husband, children, parents, friends, they all make their own choices and must face the consequences. We also need to be careful that we are not enablers, allowing them to do wrong and making excuses to cover up for them. We need tough love that helps them to accept responsibility for their own behavior and actions.

How To Change My Outlook On Today

1. Stop and smell the roses. Take time to enjoy today and don't worry about "if onlys."
2. Don't allow others to impose their moods on you. Choose your own emotions; set your own thermostat.
3. Realize that you are not responsible for the actions of others.
4. Remember that this is the day that the Lord has made, let us rejoice and be glad in it!

Tomorrow Is Never, Never Land

Wishing on stars doesn't make dreams come true, so where does our future lie?

Our future lies in Faith. What is faith? "Faith is the substance of things hoped for, the evidence of things not seen" (Hebrews 11:1).

Faith involves **Now.** It means putting God's word into work in our life **now,** knowing that we can't change one thing of our own accord. We have got to believe that God has **all things,** under control.

I know for myself that I would never have dreamed where God would take us when I resigned my first teaching job in 1979.

We couldn't see into the future, but we knew that God was calling me to stay at home with our three-year-old daughter and our one-year-old son. We'd bought a beautiful home that took both of our incomes to maintain. We didn't want to loose it, but we took the step of faith into what we believed God was calling us to do. Within six weeks we found ourselves moving to Indianapolis, Indiana, and into full-time ministry. From there we went to Germany as missionaries, then to California where my husband taught in the Bible College and was on staff at one of our largest churches, and ultimately we moved to Wisconsin to Pastor.

Not every step has been easy. There have been times of frustration and financial struggles, but God has always provided for us. There have been times when people failed us and times when we failed ourselves in decisions that we have made, but we have kept the faith and God has carried us through.

Our faith must be in Jesus and His ability to keep us! Our dreams for the future must be founded on more than wishful thinking. We have a blessed hope in the return of Jesus, but God's word says we must "occupy" until He comes. "For I know the thoughts that I think toward you, saith the LORD, thoughts of peace, and not of evil, to give you an expected end. Then shall ye call upon me, and ye shall go and pray unto me, and I will hearken unto you. And ye shall seek me, and find me, when ye shall search for me with all your heart" (Jeremiah 29:11-13).

So, lay down your past, enjoy your present and allow God to take care of your future!

Chapter Six

For Bitter or Better

Have you noticed today how some people seem to walk around with a chip on their shoulder just waiting for someone to knock it off? As the kids say, "They have an *attitude*."

Everyone is a victim today. Everyone wants their rights. If someone hurts them or offends them, they want to hurt back. They want to make them "pay." They want to offend them, as they've been offended.

The business world has developed Assertive Training Classes, designed to teach you to get and keep the upper hand so that you're never at any one else's mercy. They teach you to be forceful, to push your own agenda regardless of others ideas or feelings. Even fast food ads tell you to *"Have it your way!"* Many people today just plain have an attitude and the world encourages them to do so!

Zig Ziglar, a popular motivational speaker, says that we need a "checkup from the neck up!" He says we need to "Get rid of our stink'in think'in!"

Attitude is something we deal with on a daily basis. Our attitude affects how we act and react in life. It affects the things we do, the things we say and the responses we make to thousands of situations in any given day. What drives you crazy today may not bother you tomorrow; it all depends on your attitude or your frame of mind at the given moment.

Some offenses are very minor. You consider the source, realize the culprit is having a bad day, brush it off and go on your merry way. However, not all offenses are quite as simple to deal with. Some offenses cut to the core. They destroy your love, your hope, your faith and your trust. They seek to destroy the very foundation of your existence.

We've all been there. We've *all* been offended. Some have bounced back. Others are still wounded.

If you've never experienced what I'm talking about, you will someday. You will face an offense so great that you won't be able to think of anything else. You will wonder how you can even go on with your life. You *will* be offended.

God has designed tools to help you get through excruciating offences. Tools that will help you deal with any situation you may currently be going through or something you may face in the future, because *offences will come*.

"Woe unto the world because of offences! *for it must needs be* that offences come; but woe to that man by whom the offence cometh!" (Matthew 18:7).

"Then said he unto the disciples, It is impossible but that offences will come: but woe unto him, through whom they come!" (Luke 17:1).

Impetuous Peter once asked the Lord, "Well, how many times do I have to forgive my brother, seven times?" He probably thought that was an incredulous amount.

What did Jesus respond with? "No Peter, you need to forgive them seventy times seven!"

Satan uses whatever device he can to draw us away from God. One device that he uses very effectively is offenses. Some offenses have literally paralyzed people. They were so hurt and devastated that their life was basically frozen in time.

I'll never forget the first time I met Annie Fitch. Annie was a big-boned, tall woman in her sixties, with rounded hunched over shoulders. Her scraggly hair was pulled back to reveal a toothless grin. This was hardly the robust, beautiful lady that had once been engaged. When her fiancé broke up with her, her life came to a standstill. She fell into a deep depression that never released its powerful grip on her. She became a recluse, choosing to stay home with her parents rather than continue to work at the promising job that she held. As far as she was concerned, her life was over.

One author, John Bevere, calls offenses *The Bait of Satan*. In the Greek, the language the New Testament was written in, an offense is described as a trap, a snare, cause of displeasure or sin, occasion to fall or stumble, an offense is a thing that offends, a stumbling block.

When you think of it, traps have two components: they are hidden and they are baited. Offenses are subtle deceptions. They are hidden in places and circumstances that we would never expect and baited with things that frequently are our weaknesses.

Satan uses offenses to trap people, to shift their focus off God and to put it on their hurt, their wound, and their problem.

So the question isn't, "Will I be offended?" But rather, "How will I respond to offenses? What will my attitude be?"

John Bevere tells the story of men catching monkeys in Malaysia. The men set traps but the monkeys were too smart for them and never went in the cages. The men decided to try a new tactic. They put the bait in the cage and closed the door. The monkeys thought they were safe because the cage door was closed, so they put their arms through the bars and grabbed the bait. The bait was too large to fit through the bars and they refused to let go of the bait in their hands, so the hunters were able to go right up to them and capture them!

The same thing happens to us in regard to offenses. Satan baits the trap with some situation that bothers us or offends us. If we fall for it and don't deal properly with it, we can be caught in the devil's snare and our soul can be destroyed.

Look at the trap he set for Job. Everything he had; riches, houses, animals, even his children, were all destroyed in a matter of hours. His wife, feeling her own agony and seeing the agony of her husband, told Job to curse God and die. But scripture tells us that Job maintained his integrity with God and through it all, did not succumb to the bait of Satan that could have destroyed his soul.

Offended people produce much fruit: hurt, anger, outrage, jealousy, resentment, strife, bitterness, hatred and envy. They respond to situations with insults, verbal attacks and the wounding of others. They thrive on division, separation, broken relationships, betrayal and backsliding: ***and*** they feel justified in doing so. Because they have been hurt, without even realizing it, they go on to hurt others who had nothing to do with hurting them.

A couple of years ago I went through a period of time where I found myself being very negative, critical and non-cooperative. My family, especially my husband, became very frustrated with me. I knew I was edgy but I didn't realize how I was coming across to my family.

Finally my husband confronted me with, "Okay, what's going on?" I honestly didn't know what was going on! After much prayer, God revealed to me that I had been offended little by little by a series of events that had happened. I was allowing myself to respond with a very negative attitude. I wasn't necessarily responding negatively to those who had "offended" me, I was responding negatively to those closest to me, those who loved me the most.

When God revealed to me what was happening, I repented for allowing the offending situations to get to me. I asked God to help me to be aware of situations that I might not handle appropriately and to help me to have the right attitude in all things. I also apologized to my family and asked them to forgive me. Believe me, it made all the difference in the world! No longer did I allow things to bind me and bombard my heart and mind with unpleasing thoughts. God freed me to once again enjoy the peace of mind that only He can give.

We are all vulnerable, but Pastor's wives seem especially open to attack. Parishioners say very cutting and critical things to a Pastor's wife that they would never dream of saying to their Pastor. Pastor's wives often don't feel they can defend themselves. Many times they don't share these negative things with their husband because they do not want it to bother them. Internalizing negative comments coupled with the demands on their time, relationships and finances can cause a powder keg to develop without her even being aware that there is a serious problem.

Unfortunately, it is usually the people we are closest to that can hurt us the most. The emotional attachment we feel toward loved ones, those we have nurtured, been intimate with and bonded with, seem to offend us the deepest. Lawyers say that the most bitter cases they deal with are those of divorce. Historians tell us that the bloodiest wars that are ever fought, are civil wars.

So what is it that keeps us from letting go of our offenses? *Pride!* We don't want anyone to think they have gotten the best of us. Pride keeps us from admitting there is a problem in the first place, yet it seethes on the inside. Pride causes us to feel as if we are the "victims" in many circumstances.

Categories of Offenses

There are two basic categories of offenses:
- Those who *truly* have been treated unfairly and have been offended.
- Those who *believe* that they have been treated unfairly.

Read very carefully, and think about the second statement above. Many people are offended because of what they perceive happened to them. Either they draw conclusions from inaccurate information, or the information is correct but their conclusion is distorted. It may not have really happened in the manner that they think it happened, but they become embittered none-the-less.

As I said before, we *are* going to be offended. We must ask ourselves: What are we going to do about it? How are we going to respond?

Last year we had a situation happen that was very frustrating. It seemed like it was one of those tests that God sends you through just to see how you will handle it! I had returned a laptop computer to the manufacturer to have some work done on it. When it didn't arrive for quite some time, I called the company to see why the delay. They informed me that it should have been delivered to my home at least a month earlier. They had completed the repairs within twenty-four hours and it had been sent back to us. They decided to make an inquiry with the shipping company and found that our neighbor had received our computer and signed for it over a month earlier! A neighbor who had not spoken to us for over three years because of another situation! A neighbor who wouldn't even wave when we passed her on our lane!

To make a long story short, when we did get the computer back, absolutely nothing worked! The hard drive was crashed and the computer had to be returned to the manufacturer to be completely refurbished!

When I first found out where the computer was, guess how I felt like responding! You're right! I thought, "Boy I should march right up there and give her a piece of my mind!" But I didn't! What I did do was pray for her! She is a very lonely woman who feels like everyone is out to get her. In her own way, she felt she was getting revenge for the way people treat her. It is interesting to note that this lady has no friends. Her only child, a daughter, left home in high school and they no longer speak to one another. This same lady once told someone that when she dies she wants to come back as a bird so she can (poop) on everyone that has (pooped) on her. How very sad to think that anyone can become so bitter.

So Why Do We Have Offenses?

Jesus said, "I counsel of thee to buy of me gold tried in the fire..." (Revelations 3:18). Gold, free of alloys and impurities, is soft and pliable. God wants our heart to be soft and pliable to Him, not hard! Impurities are what make gold hard. God puts us through the fire and *if we allow him to*, He refines us with afflictions, trials and tribulations. The heat of the trials separates the dross and impurities from our lives. It takes the impurities of unforgiveness, strife, anger, revenge, envy and hatred out of our heart.

You can't see the impurities of gold until it is tried in the fire. We don't *really* know how we will respond to trials and offenses until we go through their fire.

God always sees the impurities. He allows us to go through trials so that impurities can come to the surface, we can repent of them and receive His forgiveness and purification.

When we are offended, our tendency is to see ourselves as victims and blame those who hurt us. We then justify our bitterness, unforgiveness, and all the other junk when it surfaces. God wants us to see our own condition. We can only be released from the trap when we realize who is really holding us there. Just as the prodigal son "came to himself," we have to "***come to ourselves.***"

Do you remember those woven straw finger holders we used to get at carnivals? You put a finger in each end and then tried to pull them out. They were stuck weren't they? No matter how hard you tried, you just couldn't get them out until you did the opposite of what you thought you should do, which was push your fingers towards one another. The same is true spiritually. When we defend our position, our "right" to be offended, we draw the trap tighter. When we give our situation to God to deal with, we release the stronghold and are freed from the trap!

Have you ever thought what it would be like if we didn't have any expectations of anyone else? If we had no expectations on others, we wouldn't be offended or let down, would we?

Jesus told us that many would be offended. "And then shall many be offended, and shall betray one another, and shall hate one another. And many false prophets shall rise, and shall deceive many. And because iniquity shall abound, the love of many shall wax cold. But he that shall endure unto the end, the same shall be saved" (Matthew 24: 10-13).

He told us to love our enemies, "But I say unto you, Love your enemies, bless them that curse you, do good to them that hate you, and pray for them which despitefully use you, and persecute you..." (Matthew 5:44).

From personal experience, I would have to say that most of our offenses probably come from family members, brothers and sisters in Christ and leaders in the church. "A brother offended is harder to be won than a strong city: and their contentions are like the bars of a castle" (Proverbs 18:19).

Genesis 50 gives the account of Joseph, a young man whose brothers hated him and decided to kill him but ended up selling him to slave traders. He ended up in prison through no fault of his own, but eventually became second in command in Pharaoh's Egypt. Many years later, he came face to face with his brothers. They shook in their boots when they realized who they were standing before. But, Joseph knew that God had allowed it all to happen for a purpose. His response to his brothers was, "But as for you, you meant evil against me, but God meant it for good."

Many people become angry with God when something happens in their life and they feel that God could and should have prevented the situation but didn't. Their anger separates them from the very source that desires to comfort them and to heal their broken heart and wounded spirit.

God said that we go through trials to "perfect" us, to "refine" us as pure gold. Always remember, no one can take you out of the will of God, only you yourself can do that. Satan has his greatest heyday when a person becomes angry with God and chooses to defile themselves.

"Submit yourselves therefore to God. Resist the devil, and he will flee from you" (James 4:7).

"There hath no temptation taken you but such as is common to man: but God is faithful, who will not suffer you to be tempted above that ye are able; but will with the temptation also make a way to escape, that ye may be able to bear it" (I Corinthians 10:13). We *resist* the devil by refusing to be offended.

Joseph's problem was with his brothers. He refused to allow what they had done to him to destroy his love for them or his love for God. He put things in the light of God's word and will for his life and regardless of what happened, allowed God to help him go on and do his best in every situation.

David's problem was with King Saul, his spiritual leader and father image. Saul was the first king of Israel. God chose Saul to lead Israel and he did a very good job until a young man named David came on the scene.

Israel was doing battle with the Philistines. But they were fearful and afraid. They were "shaking in their boots." The Philistines were giants and none of Israel's soldiers were willing to take the threatening challenge handed out by Goliath: "And he stood and cried unto the armies of Israel, and said unto them, Why are ye come out to set your battle in array? am not I a Philistine, and ye servants to Saul? choose you a man for you, and let him come down to me. If he be able to fight with me, and to kill me, then will we be your servants: but if I prevail against him, and kill him, then shall ye be our servants, and serve us. And the Philistine said, I defy the armies of Israel this day; give me a man, that we may fight together. When Saul and all Israel heard those words of the Philistine, they were dismayed, and greatly afraid" (I Samuel 17: 9-11).

David couldn't stand to see the armies of Israel challenged in such a manner, so he took his slingshot, got five smooth stones from the brook and went after the giant. He slew the giant with the help of the Lord and went on to be the greatest warrior in Israel.

Saul became jealous to the point that his heart turned to stone and his entire focus of life became bent on destroying David. He was angry that Israel looked to David as a mighty warrior. Saul wanted the credit and admiration.

Saul was a selfish leader. Unfortunately, like Saul, there are still selfish leaders today who are only concerned about their own goals. They view God's people as resources to serve *their* own personal vision rather than the vision as the vehicle to serve the people. They feel that the success of their vision justifies the cost of wounded and shattered people. Justice, mercy, integrity and love are compromised for their own success. They make decisions based on money, numbers and results. They feel people are expendable because the are "furthering the gospel. After all, they have a church to protect."

These men recognize godly qualities in people and are willing to *use* them as long as it personally benefits them. They consider people simply human resources to be used and disposed of when their usefulness is gone or they appear to be receiving more glory than the leader.

Men who are "serving a vision" are not serving God. They are serving their own ego. Just as Saul, they are suspicious of young men because they are personally insecure in their own calling. This breeds jealousy and pride.

Saul enjoyed David's success *until* he perceived it as a threat to himself, then he demoted David and watched for a reason to destroy him. David searched his heart to make sure that he was right in his actions. People who were rejected by their father or their leader tend to take all the blame on themselves. They become imprisoned by tormenting thoughts of, "What did I do?" They constantly try to prove their innocence to their leaders. Unfortunately, the more they try to prove their innocence, the more they feel rejected.

We once saw a minister that was resigning his church. The Assistant Pastor was his most likely replacement. The congregation loved the Assistant Pastor. He had developed a very vibrant youth group that was approaching adulthood. For some reason the Pastor did not want this young man to take the church so he rigged the election and did all sorts of things to discourage the congregation from voting for the assistant. Because the young man kept a right spirit about the situation, God intervened and a man from another state invited him to come to assist him in a very large church. Even though one man meant it for evil, God meant it for good. Had this young man become bitter over the situation, I doubt that he would be in the ministry today.

Many young men are called to assist older men or to come to spend a period of time before the church would be turned over to them. We experienced this first hand. A Pastor we had known for years asked that we come to assist him. He said that he was really "burnt out" and needed help. He alluded to the fact that he would be retiring in a few years. He told us that he couldn't give us the money to move, but he could loan us the money and when my husband became Pastor, the debt would be erased.

We felt very strongly that it was the will of God to go there. Within a few months the Pastor was quite "revived" and decided that he could pastor another ten years! In the meantime, we were unable to find jobs to support our family and finances were very tight. The church was not able to give us any money because it was small. A family in the church felt lead to give us one hundred dollars a month, which my husband cleared with the pastor, and it literally bought our groceries. The Pastor, without our knowing at the time, refused to allow my husband to preach at other churches. Protocol stated that if a pastor wanted someone else's assistant to preach in their church, that they would clear it through the local pastor. In most situations, this is rarely refused. This man, knowing our financial need, refused to consent to our ministering in other churches.

When we had been there almost a year, church members began approaching my husband and asking when the Pastor was going to resign. Because we were not at liberty to share anything with them, coupled with the fact that the pastor was "revived" and planning to stay another ten years, we realized it was time to leave. We immediately made arrangements to pay back the loan and began seeking God as to what we were to do.

When we told the pastor we were leaving, he was very angry with us. He would not allow us to say good-bye to the church. We were told not to come to church the next day. We later heard that he told people that we took tithe money from people in the church and that we never paid back the money for our moving expenses.

We had a choice as to how we were going to respond. Many emotions come into play when you are treated like this. You are hurt, you are angry, you are confused. And, if you are not careful, you will respond in a way that will destroy your spirit, your witness and your soul.

David had several opportunities to kill Saul, but he knew that he had to let God deal with his enemy. Today we don't try to "kill" people physically, but we do try to kill them with our tongue. When we try to "get back" at someone, even though what we speak is truth, we go against God's principles. "Dearly beloved, avenge not yourselves, but rather give place unto wrath: for it is written, Vengeance is mine; I will repay, saith the Lord" (Romans 12:19).

We try to avenge ourselves for selfish reasons. What we have to understand is that judgement will come, but it needs to come from God. Don't let it be by your hand. Humility and refusing to avenge ourselves, are the keys that free us from the prison of offense. When we humble ourselves, we can truly love those who offended us, and desire the best for them.

God tests his servants with obedience. He deliberately places situations in our path where we would look justified in defending ourselves. People may even encourage us to defend ourselves. But if we retain our integrity with God, He will bring us forth as "gold, tried in the fire."

Some people, who see problems coming, leave. They go somewhere else to avoid the situation, never maturing to the point where God can use them and develop them. The character development that comes only as they work through conflicts with others, is lost as the cycle of offense begins again. People who are unwilling to remain in a situation long enough for God to refine them, become "Spiritual Vagabonds." Leaving the situation is not the answer. When something is not dealt with properly and unforgiveness remains, every "next" relationship will be hindered because everything is strained through that offense -- the next church, next job, next marriage....

I heard the story of a man who was moving to town. He wanted to know how things were in the town so he thought he would take a trip to the local barber. When he sat in the chair, he told the barber that he was thinking of moving to that town and wanted to know how the people were.

"Tell me," the visitor inquired, "Are the people in this town cranky and hard to get along with? Are they gossipy and nosey?"

"Well," answered the barber, "tell me now, just how are the people in the town you come from?"

"You know, the town I come from, the people are gossipy and nosey. They are just downright mean and hard to get along with!" the man said.

"Well," said the wise barber, "that's exactly how the people are here."

Later that day, another man came into the barbershop and asked the same question, "You know, I'm thinking of moving to this town and I was just wondering, how are the people here?"

"Well," said the barber, "how are the folks in the town you're coming from?"

"Oh, the people in the town I'm coming from are wonderful! They are kind and considerate. They try to watch out for each other and everyone is just so friendly!"

"You know," the barber responded, "folks in this town are just like that."

The wise barber knew that the way each man evaluated their present situation, is the how they would appraise their next situation.

Trials and Tests Reveal the Heart

Trials and tests "locate" a person spiritually. They reveal the true condition of the heart.

Some people believe God owes them something. When things don't go the way they think they should, they get mad at Him. Offenses will reveal the weakness and breaking points in our lives. Offenses will eventually purge those who are not truly planted in Jesus. Job had every opportunity to be offended by God, but he maintained the position, that everything he owned had been obtained by God's help, so how could he be angry when God took it back.

Jesus himself offended many people. He offended his own family. Many disciples left him because of his preaching. Jesus offends people today when He doesn't do what they *think* He should do and *when* they think He should do it! "And blessed is he, whosoever shall not be offended in me" (Matthew 11:6).

Again, we *will* be offended. When you are offended, what will your response be? Will you harbor it deep in your soul? Will you allow it to "color" and "stain" everything you do? "Great peace have they which love thy law: and nothing shall offend them" (Psalms 119:165).

Not dealing with offences properly, creates a wall that separates you from God's presence. It becomes a stronghold that will make you bitter. A root of bitterness will spring up that will defile you and destroy you. It will make you hate people. "Looking diligently lest any man fail of the grace of God; lest any root of bitterness springing up trouble you, and thereby many be defiled" (Hebrews 12:15). Bitterness is unfulfilled revenge. Roots that are not pulled out quickly and are allowed time to grow, get entangled with other roots and grow deep, making it even more difficult to pull them up. Eventually you reap a harvest of anger, resentment, jealousy, hatred, strife and discord (spoken of as evil fruits in Matthew 7:19-20).

God wants us to respond to offenses as little children do. They get upset with one another but their anger doesn't last. They quickly forgive and go on. Their parents may still be upset about the situation, but the children have completely forgotten it.

If you feel you have been offended, you must immediately forgive! Satan wants you to think people are your enemies. He wants you to let the wound fester. He wants the wound to become like gangrene that eats you alive. His entire mission is to steal, to kill and to destroy the very existence of your life. Unforgiveness allows a stronghold to develop in your life.

God wants the wound to be cleansed so it can heal. Antiseptic disinfects and cleanses. It may sting at first, but it makes things heal much faster and leaves fewer scars.

Take the time to read the story of the debtors, found in Matthew 18. Jesus said that if we were not willing to forgive, we would not be forgiven. God only forgives us to the degree that we have forgiven those who have hurt us. (Mark 11:24-26; Matthew 6:14-15; Luke 6:37; Matthew 6:12)

Unforgiveness will keep you from maturing in God.

The way we forgive, is the way we will be forgiven. The love and forgiveness of God is the key to freedom from the baited trap of offense. True forgiveness is relinquishing your right or desire to hurt the one who has hurt you. When you have truly forgiven someone, you can pray for him. You can bless them. You *can* do good to them as Matthew 5: 43-44 instructs us to, even if they hate you, even if they persecute you. **Forgiveness is a choice!**

How about you? Have you had a chip on your shoulder? Is there someone in your life that has offended you so deeply that you don't believe you can ever forgive them? Regardless of the situation, whether it is recent or in the past, God **can** help you to forgive them.

Picture the person in your mind. Ask God to release them from the blame for what they have done to you. In your heart and mind, cancel the debt they owe you. Take the chip off your shoulder and lay it at the foot of the cross, the cross Jesus died on to make atonement for **your** sins.

Ask God to cleanse your mind from constantly dwelling on the thoughts that encompass the situation. And when Satan comes to bring it up, rebuke him in the name of Jesus Christ, reminding him that the situation is covered by the blood of Jesus!

Chapter Seven
Treasures of the Heart

Where is our treasure? What is our treasure? What is the *only* thing on this earth that we will take to heaven with us? Jesus said, "For where your treasure is, there will your heart be also" (Matthew 6:21).

Our families and friends are our treasures. They are the *only things* we will take to heaven with us. II Corinthians tells us, "But we have this treasure in earthen vessels...." These are the earthen vessels that can contain the Spirit of God.

In the previous chapter, I mentioned that offenses often come from those that are the closest to us. Because we have invested so much of ourselves in them, when they hurt us, or when you hurt them, those hurts are the deepest. Many offenses can be avoided when we understand our own personality's strengths and weaknesses and those of our family members and friends.

Each of us has a unique temperament or personality. Tim LaHaye, in *The Spirit-Controlled Temperament* says, "This basic temperament is called several things in the Bible, "the natural man," "the flesh," and "the old man," to name a few. It is the basic impulse of our being that seeks to satisfy our wants. It is the combination of inborn traits that sub-consciously affects our behavior. Our personality is the outward expression of ourselves."

Many contemporary Christian psychologists believe that children arrive fully equipped with a God-given personality "bent" at birth. Scripture teaches us that as parents, we are to "Train up a child in the way he should go: and when he is old, he will not depart from it" (Proverbs 22:6). In Hebrew, the phrase, "in the way he should go," actually refers to the "bent or bend" in which he should go. In other words, God has already given them a "bent" and we are to train them in that "bent."

The study of personalities is not new. Hippocrates, the father of modern medicine, noted four distinct personalities and named them over 3,500 years ago. Some modern researchers have coined new terms for them and many tests have been designed to identify the basic personalities and their blends. Businesses have found that particular personalities are better suited for specific jobs; and they hire accordingly.

Florence Littauer, Dr. Jim Dobson, Dr. Kevin Leaman, Gary Smalley, and Dr. Tim LaHaye have been researching, writing and speaking about personalities for many years. Gary Smalley says, "In sharing this across the country, we've seen the resulting insight bring many couples and families closer together almost instantly!" Understanding personalities has proven very effective in our own family and has literally transformed some relationships in our church.

When we understand people and their personality "bents," we can interact with them in ways that are encouraging and non-threatening. Also we can avoid being offended by things they do that would normally drive us up a wall!

The more we learn to treasure our loved ones' natural abilities, bents and talents, especially if they are different from ours, the more we can minister to them. When we make demands on people that go against their natural bent, we push the person away from us. Some personalities tend to be "hard" on others so they offend people without realizing it.

Parents need to know how to work with their child's personality to help them grow spiritually. Parents need to know how their own personality reacts with each individual child's personality. Some children cower under certain personalities of their parents. Some *parents* cower under their children's personalities! Problems arise when parents don't enforce rules, especially with particular personalities. Other children need very few rules because they will seldom disobey you.

A family of four can very conceivably have four very distinct personalities living under their roof! We have three children and all three are very different. Growing up: one was choleric, one was phlegmatic and one was sanguine. Treating all of them the same would have been a misnomer. They each had different emotional needs and different discipline needs.

Personality conflicts *do* exist, but a little study on the subject can go a long way in resolving them.

In the remainder of this chapter, I will share with you the various personalities and their strengths and weaknesses. As you read through them, you will be able to pick out your dominant characteristics. You may find that you are a blend of two or three personality types. It is not uncommon to find that your weaknesses are one type and your strengths another. You will also be able to pick out the basic characteristics of each of your family members. (If you are interested in taking a personality test, I have included information in the back of this book as to how you can obtain a very valuable and informative test booklet.)

There are many good books on the subject. I have already mentioned several authors that address this issue and offer various quizzes and tests that you can take to more specifically determine your personality type. These sources and others are listed in the chapter entitled *Readers are Leaders.*

Sanguine
Descriptive Keys

Energetic/Enthusiastic	Cheerful and Bubbly
Emotional	Charms others to work
Disorganized/Forgetful	Loves bright colors

Strengths

Friendly	Convincing
Loves people	Cheerful
Animated	Carefree
Warm	Creative and colorful
Funny	Responsive
Doesn't hold grudges	Generous
Playful	Compassionate
Volunteers and gets others to volunteer

Weaknesses

Too happy for some	Compulsive talker
Exaggerates	Doesn't follow through
Appears egotistical	Seems phony to some
Can't remember names	Undisciplined
Interrupts and doesn't listen	Repeats stories
Restless	Permissive/flirty
Makes excuses	Inconsistent

Needs

Affirmation and approval	Teaching on faithfulness
Help in getting founded in God	To develop self-discipline
Guidelines and boundaries	Organization

Choleric

Descriptive Keys

Decisive
Powerful
Direct

Dominant
Independent
Strong-willed

Strengths

Leader
Decisive
Adventurous
Visionary
Positive
Optimistic
Independent
Organizes well

Persuasive
Courageous
Competitive
Self-confident
Bold
Productive
Practical

Weaknesses

Crafty
Cold
Argumentative
Impatient
Inconsiderate
Unsympathetic
Bossy

Short tempered
Opinionated
Unforgiving
Revengeful
Unaffectionate
Never Wrong

Needs

To get credit for their work
Tolerance for others
Not to overpower others
To slow down, not be a workaholic

Patience
Give forgiveness
Compassion for others

Phlegmatic

Descriptive Keys

Sympathetic
Status Quo
Stable

Peaceable
Quiet
Easy going

Strengths

Calm/Peaceable
Relaxed
Conservative
Quiet but witty
Kind
Steady
Supportive
Content

Serves Others
Dependable
Practical
Gentle
Patient
Friendly
Diplomatic

Weaknesses

Unmotivated
Indecisive
Too compromising
Selfish
Mumbler
Self-protective
Stubborn
Worrier

Procrastinator
Spectator
Hates change
Self righteous
Fearful
Unenthusiastic
Eager to rest

Needs

Motivation
To get involved and serve others
To prioritize and do it!

Respect in relationships
To release bitterness
To be valued by others

Melancholy

Descriptive Keys

Controlled
Conscientious
Competent

Compliant
Analytical
Talented

Strengths

Gifted
Artistic
Self-sacrificing
Idealistic
Creative
Dutiful and responsible
Behaved
Respectful

Diligent worker
Loyal
Thoughtful
Deep thinker
Very detail oriented
Planner
Organizer

Weaknesses

Martyr syndrome
Touchy/Moody
Fearful
Fussy
Inferiority complex
Revengeful
Prone to depression

Self-centered
Critical
Unforgiving
Insecure
Overly sensitive
Unsociable
Withdrawn

Needs

To lighten up on self and family
To give problems totally to God
Not be so legalistic
Focus on others rather than self

To rejoice
Enjoy life more
Learn to give affection

Sanguine

Sanguines are a "party waiting to happen!" They are talkers, outgoing, optimistic and happy-go-lucky. They are emotional and demonstrative. They are people oriented and are encouragers. They love to tell stories and may physically hold onto their listener. They tend to be disorganized. Their greatest fear is that of rejection. Their favorite line is "Let's Party!" Their personality role is that of the "star." They tend to manipulate conversations. An animal used to depict them is the fun loving otter. One children's author called her ***Miss Sunshine***.

Sanguines are very popular people. They make friends easily and everyone thinks they are his best friend. This hurts some people when they realize that the sanguine may not even remember them! Sanguines feed on compliments and wilt under criticism. They tend to have problems handling money—they like to spend it!

They would rather cook gourmet meals for entertaining than everyday meals for their family. They need to be careful because they are the most vulnerable in sexual temptations. Because they tend to flirt, they often send the wrong message to people of the opposite sex.

They frequently loose things like keys, checkbooks, passports, etc., and forget important things like picking up their kids at school or forgetting to take them home after church. One time our daughter Sharon wanted to run to the store before dinner on Sunday. She assured me that she just had to pick up one thing and she would be home. Just as we sat down to the dinner table, she called. She couldn't find the keys to her brother's car. She had no idea where they were. She had retraced her steps several times, and looked in the windows of the locked car and couldn't find them. Finally, she checked a bin of panty hose that she had looked through and found that she had laid them in the bin as she looked through the pile.

One lady went to the mall. When she went to put her items in the car, it was nowhere to be found. She contacted mall security and they helped her search the parking lot. Concluding that her car must have been stolen, they called the police and filed a stolen vehicle report. She proceeded to turn it into her insurance company and within a month, she received a check for the stolen car. A few days later she received a phone call from Sears. The automobile service manager said, "Lady, when are you going to pick up this car? It's been at least a month since you brought it in to get new tires."

When Sanguines do embarrassing things, instead of keeping it to themselves, they tell everyone! They tend to be impetuous and put their foot in their mouth much like Peter did!

Jesus was very much a Sanguine. He loved to be with people. He had compassion toward others. He was an encourager. He was a storyteller. He was friendly, cheerful, warm, responsive, and he didn't hold grudges.

Choleric

Cholerics are considered born leaders. They are the extrovert, the driver, the doer.

They have a very strong will. They tend to be impatient and are always in a time crunch. They seek to be in authority. They are goal oriented and are not easily discouraged. They seem to thrive on opposition. Their greatest fear is that of being taken advantage of. Their favorite line is "Let's do it my way!" Their personality role is that of the worker. The animal that is often used to describe their personality is the lion. One children's author called her **Miss Bossy.**

Cholerics are self-reliant. They like to direct things and be in control and are often managers. They don't lead people as much as they drive them. They tend to be hard on their family members and co-workers. They like power and can appear intimidating to others. The **job** is more important than the people are. After all, if no one wants to help, they can do it themselves. To the choleric, life is a series of problems that they need to solve or challenges they need to meet. They tend to be workaholics and when they give you something to do, they expect it to be done yesterday! Their hardness sometimes leaves them isolated.

If you've read this chapter and don't believe any of what I've said, you are probably choleric!

Dr. Dobson says that the choleric child is the classic "strong-willed child" who lets his parents live in their home!

They need to learn to allow others to help with decision making. They need to slow down and learn to listen to others. They need to learn how to show love to their family and realize that developing a loving home is more effective than demanding loyalty.

Paul was a choleric. There were times when he didn't have much patience with people. He was very goal oriented. He was a leader. He was bold and he was courageous. He was visionary, persuasive and adventurous.

Jesus was very much a choleric. He is known as the "Lion of Judah." He roared as a lion when He chased the moneychangers from the temple. Jesus was bold, He was a leader, He was visionary; and He was extremely persuasive. He was not easily discouraged. He was powerful, practical and optimistic.

Phlegmatic

Phlegmatics are considered "watchers." They are faithful, tend to be introverts and are often pessimists. They are very loyal and tend to be possessive. They are very family oriented. They are slow to change and they like to avoid problems. Their greatest fear is loss of security. Their favorite line is "Let's do it the easy way!" Their personality role tends to be that of the audience. Because of their loyalty and faithfulness, they are characterized as a Golden Retriever. One children's author called her *Miss Shy*.

Above all, Phlegmatics are loyal. They have a strong need for close relationships. They have a deep need to please others and they are sensitive to hurting people. They are great listeners and their hearts are full of compassion. They are easily hurt by people that are insensitive to them. These children will be so supportive that they will mother you if you let them! They often don't feel that they are respected as they should be and often feel taken for granted. They need to learn to hold their ground on issues and not allow themselves to be manipulated. They don't like change and can become very stubborn when they see it coming on. If they are given a part in the process of making changes, they can accept it much better. They feel "used" when they have to go along with something that they had no part in discussing. They need extra time to think through major decisions. They hold stubbornly to what they feel is right.

Phlegmatics tend to be "couch potatoes." If they have to stand in line for something, you will often find them leaning on something. They would never volunteer for a leadership roll or position, but when they are pressed into it, they make very good leaders. One reason they don't volunteer to be leaders is they don't like conflict. Having to confront a Choleric is no fun!

Abraham was Phlegmatic. He was called "a friend of God." He never tried to make waves. He was a peacemaker. He was content to follow wherever God led him and he was always the diplomat. He was sympathetic to the needs of his family and took his nephew Lot with him although it hindered his progress in God's plan. He was ever faithful and loyal to God.

Jesus was the ultimate peacemaker. It is recorded that not one war took place during his earthly lifetime. With His spoken word he calmed the raging seas. He was very loyal and talked often about His family and how he loved and cared for them. He was kind and patient with everyone he met. No one could ever be a better listener than Jesus. In Matthew 11:30, He said, "For my yoke is easy, and my burden is light." He never made it hard for us to serve Him.

Melancholy

Melancholies are considered thinkers. They tend to be introverted, pessimistic and soft-spoken. They are perfectionists and tend to be too hard on themselves and others. They are very sensitive. Because they do things "by the book" they need many explanations. They are worriers so it is difficult to make decisions because they are afraid they will make a mistake. They have a tendency to judge people. Their greatest fear is that their life is out of order and that they will be criticized. Their favorite line is "Let's do it perfect!" Their personality role is that of the producer. Because they are such industrious workers, the beaver is used to represent them. One children's author called her *Miss Neat*.

Melancholies are very analytical. Surgeons are most often melancholy, spotting miniscule things and wanting to make sure things are done right. They make very good quality control people, but they can be so detail oriented that they sometimes drive other people crazy. They often talk quietly and if you ask them to repeat what they said, they talk even more softly. They find it difficult to make friends and are reserved in their relationships. They "need their space." They tend to marry late in life, if at all because they can't find the "perfect mate." They must finish a task to be at peace. They have a difficult time getting beyond things that happened in the past. If things don't go according to plan, they search their past for some secret sin that could have brought on the calamity. They dwell on the "what ifs" that take the joy out of life Melancholy children need praise and encouragement of their character as well as their accomplishments. They need to be told that they don't have to get A's in everything. Melancholy parents need to lighten up on their children. Their rooms don't have to be perfect every time you walk in the room.

Melancholies have a difficult time rounding numbers up or down. When they pay their tithes, it is ten percent to the penny. When they leave a tip, it is to the penny. They are very good at record keeping and saving money. (They are **too** good at keeping records of past hurts and personal failures.) If they are driving and they fail to come to a complete stop at an intersection, or they try to get through a yellow light but it turns red just as they pass under it, they worry themselves sick because they know they did something that they shouldn't have done. They may call a friend and ask if they should make things right by going to the police station and reporting what they did.

Moses was a melancholy. When God called Moses, he immediately gave the excuse that he was slow of speech and surely couldn't be used by God. Moses wanted a very clear plan of action because he wanted to make sure he made no mistakes. God used him to deliver His people and His law because He knew Moses would do it right.

Jesus was a melancholy. He did things "by the book." He said, "I come not to condemn the law but to fulfill it." He completed every thing He set out to do. He was a deep thinker. There were many times when He went away to be by himself to pray. There is no question about the self-sacrificing of His ministry. No man ever controlled His emotions like Jesus did, considering He could have called ten thousand angels to rescue Him from the cross, but He chose to die for you and me.

This has been a very brief overview of the four basic personalities. Again, the primary advantage of learning about personalities is to discover our most pronounced strengths and weaknesses so that with God's help we can overcome our weaknesses and take advantage of our strengths.

As you studied the personalities, if you have found some areas that need improvement, ask God to help you to develop spiritually in those areas. When we come to Him, He does not expect us to stay as He found us. He expects us to grow up in

Him. "As newborn babes, desire the sincere milk of the word, that ye may grow thereby" (I Peter 2:2). If you are constantly finding conflicts in your life as you deal with people, there are probably some things in your personality that need to "grow up."

Chapter Eight

Knit Pickers or Knit Fixers

Do you like bargains? I know some people who go shopping and they never look at the price tag, like my husband! He sees what he wants, picks it up and heads for the checkout counter. Boy not me! I look for bargains! If I find a bargain in one store, I'll challenge myself to find a better bargain in another store! Sometimes I find that I loose my first bargain in the process! But, I do like bargains!

One time I came home from shopping and told my husband, "Hon, I saved you $270.00 today!"

"$270.00," he gasped, "What on earth did you buy?"

"Nothing," I replied, "but I could have spent at least that amount!"

I like to bargain hunt, but I also shop wisely. You can buy a lot of 'bargains' that you don't need, but in doing so, you only end up wasting money. I like to purchase things that are practical, sturdy and needed. If you are handy with sewing, and you don't mind, you can purchase things at bargain prices that need minor repairs like mending a seam, sewing on a button or repairing a snag.

Once, when we were living in California, I purchased a lovely sea-foam green dress on sale. I thought it would be practical and pretty for summer. After wearing it a couple of times, I found out that it was the type of fabric that 'picks' easily. I didn't wear it for a long time because it had so many unsightly 'picks' in the fabric. Then my mother-in-law gave me the neatest little gadget, a knit fixer. Boy did that do the job! You just locate the 'pick,' put the 'knit fixer' on the snag and punch it to the other side. The snag is then pulled to the inside of the dress and no one but me knows that the pick ever existed!

Psalms tells us that we are "knit together in our mother's womb!" We know that knit fabrics can be 'picked' but I have found that in 'life,' there are snags too! Things that knick us and prick us, sometimes exposing our fragile fabric to the world. We need something to help fix the picks in our life. As Christians, we know that we can call upon God to help us, to cover our mistakes, our faults and our failures. But God has commanded us, as Christians, to cover the mistakes, faults and failures of others. "And above all things have fervent charity among yourselves for charity shall cover the multitude of sins" (I Peter 4:8).

"Let him know, that he which converteth the sinner from the error of his way, shall save a soul from death and shall hide a multitude of sins" (James 5:20).

When I study the meaning of a scripture, I like to use Strong's Concordance, Matthew Henry's Commentary and other sources, to look for the original meaning of the words. Many times there are hidden meanings of scripture. I Peter 4:8 has no hidden meanings.

Jesus is simply telling us, "I'm not the only one that should be doing the 'covering.' I'm not the only one that should be doing the 'fixing' in people's lives."

God has given us the responsibility and the privilege to help save men and women from their sins for the Kingdom of God.

In life, there are two kinds of people: Knit pickers and Knit fixers.

Some people just have a knack for going by and having something to pick at you for. They are never happy about anything you do or say. They always seem to be picking on you. They pick at your personality quirks, they pick at your family, they try to embarrass you in front of others by always correcting what you say, or they never let you finish saying anything. It's almost like they are wearing magnifying glasses so they can see and expose every miniscule flaw you have!

They're like the Pharisees, always trying to put someone else down, thinking that in doing so, they are lifting themselves up. Jesus said they're like the man who had a beam in his eye. Though he couldn't see his own faults and failures, he was determined to correct the one with the splinter in his eye, the one with the minor problems.

My husband has an aunt named Hester. She and her husband Bert would get after each other all the time. He would tell others the 'dumb' things Hester would do. One time she told him, "Bert, if it wasn't for you, everyone would think I was plumb perfect!"

Some people just have to tell everything they know. Who did what horrible thing, who said what to whom.... They have a common, fatal flaw. They can't ever really forgive people when they make a mistake, because they can't forget what they did. They bring up past faults and failures with regularity. They seek to uncover anything and everything that Jesus has covered, through repentance, with His blood.

These people are quick to argue their point, because they think they are always "right!" (Something we all fall victim to if we don't guard our heart.)

I remember one time when we were on vacation in Canada. Somehow we got on a discussion about a little stool my daughter had. I distinctly remembered that the stool had three legs, my husband was sure it had four. We "discussed" it until it became a bone of contention! I couldn't wait until we got home to prove to him that it had three legs! You guessed it—it had four legs! Why all of the fuss? I wanted to be right!

The entire book of Obadiah chastises Israel for their hardness of heart against their brothers in Judah. God told them that wanting Judah to perish was a result of their pride. He even mentioned the problem with Jonah's hardness of heart toward the Ninevites and his unwillingness to forgive them. Obadiah 11 says, "For thy violence against thy brother Jacob, shame shall cover thee, and thou shalt be cut off forever." In essence, all they were doing was "knit picking," for which they ultimately paid the heavy price of being cut off from the presence of God.

Then there are the 'knit fixers.' They always have a kind word to say. They are always trying to encourage you. They are always willing to listen, and you know that what you are saying isn't going to be shouted from the rooftops.

They look past your faults. They look beyond your past. They not only allow you to grow spiritually, but they help you as well. 'Knit fixers' look through rose-colored glasses, just as Jesus did when He saw you. They look through the eyes of faith that see the end from the beginning. They lift you up when you falter. They help to bind your spiritual wounds and give you time to heal. They don't try to scar you further by pulling off the scabs before they are healed. They tell you to go, and sin no more. They cover your multitude of sins with their love, just as Jesus did for the woman that was taken in adultery.

Well, what are you? Are you a 'knit picker' or a 'knit fixer'?

Unfortunately, as wives and mothers, we tend to be knit pickers! We have every excuse in the book to justify our actions. Sometimes we pick and prod at our loved ones until they can't stand to be around us anymore!

God is telling us that He wants us to be 'knit fixers'. He wants us to love others and to help as many people as we can, to cover as many sins as we can. I am not talking about blatant sins that have never been repented of and/or continue to be exercised in the lives of people. I am talking about sins that have been washed by the blood of Jesus in repentance. Those whose sincere desire is to follow after Jesus, but as a baby, they make mistakes along the way. Those who are endeavoring to become like Christ as they grow in Him.

"Beloved, let us love one another: for love is of God; and everyone that loveth is born of God, and knoweth God. He that loveth not knoweth not God; for God is love. In this was manifested the love of God toward us, because that God sent his only begotten Son into the world, that we might live through him. Herein is love, not that we love God, but that he loved us and sent his Son to be the propitiation for our sin. Beloved, if God so loved us, we ought also to love one another. No man hath seen God at any time. If we love one another, God dwelleth in us, and his love is perfected in us" (I John 4:7-12).

Determine in your heart, that from this day forward, with God's help, you are going to be a 'knit fixer!' You are going to be an encourager! You are going to be the best spiritual cheerleader you can be, to spur souls into the Kingdom! Amen!

Chapter Nine
Returning To First Love

I would like for you to spend a couple of minutes and take a trip down memory lane. If you would like to get out a pencil and paper and respond to a few questions it will help you to focus on a particular topic that is of the utmost importance.

I want you to think of the first time you realized that you truly loved the man you married. Think of the things that made you "fall in love" with him. What did he do that swept you off your feet? How did you feel when he asked you to marry him?

Next, if you are a mother, I want you to think of your first thoughts and emotions when they placed that tiny bundle of energy in your arms just minutes after such hard labor. What were your first thoughts?

Now I want you to think about your parents. What is one really special thing that you remember them doing for you? At what point in your life did you realize that they weren't as "dumb" as you had always thought?

Now think of the first feelings and emotions you experienced when you gave your heart to God in sweet surrender.

In this chapter, I'd like to talk to you about "Returning to First Love." I've heard several messages preached about returning to our 'first love' for Christ and how important that is, but just now, for a few minutes, I would like for you to focus on the other 'first loves' in your life.

The First Love of your Husband

To me, one of the saddest things is to hear about a couple, who after having been married seven, ten, fifteen and even twenty-five years, are getting a divorce. When you talk with them, they say things like: "I never really loved him/her." "We never had anything in common." "We just stayed together because of the children."

What a sad commentary on our society. Our marriages are not prearranged as they are in some cultures. For the most part, Americans marry for "love" alone, unfortunately even when advised against it!

What happens then? I believe they loose their "first love". Perhaps they go into the marriage with unrealistic expectations that can never be met. Perhaps they allow individual desires to draw them apart. Or perhaps they just didn't take the time to nurture their relationship, for whatever reason.

A fire that is not fed will eventually go out! So it is with love.

Let's face it, it's not easy to be romantic sometimes. It's also not 'practical' at times, but it is extremely important non-the-less!

Dating should never stop! It certainly gets harder as children arrive, financial crises hit and other stresses attack the marriage, but it is so important to take the time to smell the roses!

If you are going through a time when love seems to be waning, don't give up the ship! Make a decision that whatever it takes, you are going to do your part to make it work and keep the love alive.

Find someone to talk to that you know has a good relationship in their marriage. Ask them what has worked for them. As a couple, you might want to ask an older couple to mentor you, to share things that worked in their relationship during difficult times.

I have received anonymous phone calls from ladies desiring help in this area. I try to answer their questions as discreetly as I can and suggest particular books and/or authors that I feel will help them.

Marabel Morgan in *The Total Woman* gives a fresh approach to keeping excitement in your marriage. *The Act of Marriage* by Tim LaHaye is excellent in helping couples understand intimacy as are Dr. Ed Wheat's books. Read books that help you to understand the differences in the way men and women communicate, not just in words but how they express their love to one another.

Don't let your marriage die! Return to that "First Love" and it will get better and better!

The First Love of your Children

Children who are growing into teens, aren't nearly as easy to 'love' as they were the first time you held them, are they? One Pastor said that he believes kids go brain dead between the ages of 13 and 18! Sometimes I almost have to agree! Never the less, your responsibility to love and nurture them is no less when they are at these difficult and frustrating ages. I know that when my children were in their teens that I seemed to be so involved and "busy" doing what I needed to do, just to take care of them, that I didn't take the time to spend *with* them like I should have.

Working mothers have an especially difficult task with so many demands on their lives just helping to make ends meet financially.

When I first taught this lesson, about nine years ago, I remember thinking how I longed to have more time to write. Then it dawned on me how little time I *really* had left with my children at home. I realized that they were at ages where they needed as much attention as I could give them. It made me feel good that Sharon was ten and still enjoyed being rocked occasionally, that John David was twelve and still kissed me good-bye when he got out of the car at school in front of all of his friends, and that Amy still liked to hear the stories of things she did when she was a little girl. Even though it seemed that they were so grown up and didn't need me as much, deep down on the inside, they probably needed my love and support more than ever!

Every once in a while I had to remind myself of a poem I had embroidered and hung in my baby's room many years ago:

> *Cleaning and scrubbing*
> *Can wait 'til tomorrow.*
> *For children grow up,*
> *We've learned to our sorrow.*
> *So fly away cobwebs,*
> *Dust go to sleep.*
> *I'm rocking my baby-*
> *And babies don't keep!*

You need to rock them, kiss them, hug them and talk to them as much as possible while you have them with you. The day will come all too soon when you realize that those days are gone. Their affections will be set on someone else and it will never be the same. So, enjoy every moment while you can!

Nurture them, love them, care for them, but always keep in the back of your mind the fact that when those children are gone, you will still have your husband. So don't put him on the back burner while you are caring for your children!

The First Love of your Parents

Loving our parents and respecting them is the first of the Ten Commandments with a "promise." It holds the promise of long life.

Remember the loving cards, notes and gifts you gave them as a child, and the awesome respect you had for them. As you grew older, you realized that they weren't perfect, that they made mistakes, that they were seemingly unjust at times and they weren't nearly as smart as you'd always thought they were. As you grew up you lost some of that initial respect you had for them. Think about it. If you've lost some of that awe, ask God to return you to that "first love" for your parents. Realizing that they, like you, are imperfect, will help you to love them as you did when you were a little child; when their imperfections were covered by your love.

I realize that some of you probably grew up in situations that were harsh. Not all parents really know how to be loving parents. Maybe you have a hard time relating to your parents in a positive manner. If that is your case, ask God to help you. Ask him to heal the hurts, the heartaches and the painful memories. Ask him to give you a love for your parents that covers all of their sins against you and allows you to see them through the eyes of Jesus.

The First Love of Christ

How is your current relationship with the lover of your soul? Is your heart waxing cold? Jesus said, "I would rather you be either cold or hot, but because you are lukewarm, I will spew you out of my mouth."

When we are "hot," we are on fire for God and serving him with our whole heart. When we are "cold," we are not close to God. His hope is that we will eventually become uncomfortable and miserable enough to see our need to return to his loving presence. When we are "lukewarm," we are comfortable living in a spiritual condition where we don't see the need to draw closer to God. Our conscious becomes callused and in essence, we become our own gods.

A frog that is thrown into a pan of hot water, knows he needs to take action and jumps out quickly. A frog that is placed in lukewarm water is comfortable to stay there. As the water is gradually heated to the boiling point, he doesn't see the danger and ends up being boiled alive because he was lulled into complacency. He didn't feel the need to take action. Souls who are lukewarm feel they are "okay," when they really need to "take action" spiritually and draw closer to God.

Losing our "first love" in these valuable areas of life, is actually a sign of the times "And because iniquity shall abound, the love of many shall wax cold" (Matthew 24:12).

Don't allow your marriage, your relationship with your children and your relationship with your parents to become a statistic. Allow God to speak to you, "I remember thee, the kindness of thy youth, the love of thine espousals, when thou wentest after me in the wilderness" (Jeremiah 2:2). Ask God to restore you to that first love in your relationship with your husband, your children, your parents and with God himself.

Chapter Ten

Love Languages

Keeping love "alive" in a marriage is serious business. It requires time, effort, commitment and a desire to meet the other person's needs.

One of the number one reasons sited for divorce today is lack of communication. How can that be you say? We both speak the same language. We should be able to understand each other! You may speak only one verbal language, but you "communicate" in many different ways. You communicate in the tone of your voice, in your body language and the way in which you demonstrate love to one another.

What would your home be like if one morning you woke up to find that everyone spoke a different language? You spoke French, your husband spoke Mandarin Chinese, your son spoke Swahili and your daughter spoke Russian. I dare say it would be quite difficult to "communicate" with one another!

If you really loved one another, you would do your best to work together on figuring out what the other person was saying. You would have patience and realize that in time you would learn to communicate. Either you would learn their language or they would learn your language.

Dr. Gary Chapman, in his book *The Five Love Languages*, teaches that each of us speaks different emotional love languages. You may speak the same verbal language but the way you demonstrate and understand "love" is often "spoken" in different ways. Just as you have a primary spoken language, you have a primary love language. Your primary love language is what comes natural to you. It is what you do automatically. The conflicts come when your spouse does not speak the same love language that you do.

You think you are showing them love by the things you do or say, but you see no response or appreciation from them and you don't understand. You work hard all week cooking and cleaning, taking care of the children and fixing delicious meals, but your spouse rarely acts like he notices! You interpret that to mean that he doesn't really love you or appreciate you. On they other hand, he feels the same way. He plans little surprises or get-a-ways to spend quality time with you and you respond as though it was a waste of your time. He interprets your actions to say you don't want to spend time with him. You are each expressing love to the other, but it is like you are speaking to one another in a foreign language. Neither understands the other. It is not something that is done intentionally. It is an aspect of miscommunication.

Most people never understand what the real problem is. They go through the relationship feeling frustrated because they don't feel their needs are being met. They don't realize their spouse is feeling the same way. As a result, they "fall out of love." They begin to withdraw from one another. They begin to emotionally separate from their spouse and if they are not careful, they will begin to look for someone else to meet their emotional needs.

It didn't start out that way. When you first began to date, it seemed that the one you loved met all of your emotional needs. You were sure that it would always continue. So what happened? Unfortunately, the euphoria of the "falling in love" experience doesn't last forever. After you are married comes the hard work of *learning* to love each other. That's when your vows kick in: For better, for worse…

Learning and understanding your primary love language helps you communicate your needs to your spouse. Learning and understanding their love language allows you to truly meet their emotional needs. This is the key to long lasting, loving marriages.

Seldom do husbands and wives have the same primary emotional love language. Just as opposites attract in personalities, it seems that opposite love languages attract as well! So what do you do? Just as you would learn a second language to communicate verbally to your loved one, you need to learn their primary love language and make it your secondary love language.

There are five basic Love Languages:
- Words of Affirmation
- Quality Time
- Receiving Gifts
- Acts of Service
- Physical Touch

Love Language #1
Words of Affirmation

Solomon, the wisest man that ever lived, wrote, "The tongue has the power of life and death" (Proverbs 18:21). Couples need to learn the power of verbally affirming each other. Verbal compliments, or words of appreciation, are powerful communicators of love.

If you feel your spouse is not responding to you; failing to meet your needs, or not doing things around the house, don't nag him. Find something he does very well and give him a verbal compliment. Don't flatter him to manipulate him into doing what you want, but rather tell him sincerely what you appreciate about him. Encourage him. Don't put him down in public. Don't feel like you have to correct every story he tells. Believe me, if his love language is "Words of Affirmation" and you become his best "cheerleader," he will do everything that he can to meet your emotional needs!

Always remember: love makes requests – not demands. Demands put your spouse in the position of a child and drive him away from you.

Encouraging words may be difficult for you to speak. It may not be your primary love language and it may take great effort on your part to learn this second language. This is especially true if you have a habit of saying critical and condemning words, but God is more than able to help you.

Love Language #2
Quality Time

Quality time is giving someone your undivided attention. It is not saying, "Uh, huh," as you continue vacuuming the carpet or peek out from behind the newspaper. It is *really* listening to someone, hearing what they have to say and not biting at the bit to get the next word in. It is being a sounding board when they have problems. It is maintaining eye contact, listening for feelings, observing body language and not interrupting! Quality conversation is a genuine desire to understand their thoughts, feelings and desires. They just need you to listen. Don't interject your own thoughts, ideas or solutions to their problem.

If this is your spouse's primary love language, establish a daily sharing time to talk about the things that happened to them that day. Be willing to do activities, just the two of you, that give you time to get away and really share thoughts and feelings with one another.

Love Language #3
Receiving Gifts

Gifts are a visual symbol of love in every culture. Receiving gifts are more important to some people than to others. People with this love language don't usually care how much you pay for something; the point is you thought enough of them to give them a gift, especially at odd times when they weren't expecting it.

If your spouse is critical of the gifts you give, than this is probably not their love language! If they complain that you never bring them flowers or candy like you used to, this **is** probably their gift.

Gift giving is one of the easiest love languages to learn. If you realize this is your spouse's need, don't wait for a special occasion, almost anything will be received as an expression of love. If you are to be an effective gift giver, you may have to change your attitude about money! Some people are spenders and some are savers. Spenders don't have any trouble buying gifts for their spouse. Savers experience emotional resistance to the idea of spending money as an expression of love, but when you think in terms of "making an investment in your relationship," you realize that you are ultimately meeting both of your needs.

Sometimes "just being there" when crises hits is a love gift. If you need your spouse to be with you during particular situations, tell him. He is not a mind reader.

If you realize this is your spouse's love language, make it a point to give him a little gift every day for a week and see what happens!

Love Language #4
Acts of Service

Acts of service are the "stuff of life." It is doing the dishes, mopping the floor, grocery shopping and taking out the garbage. If this is your gift, you express your love by doing things for your spouse that you know he would like for you to do. It could be fixing his favorite meal, wearing a certain outfit, or ironing his shirts. If this is your primary love language than you may not feel it is necessary to tell your spouse you love him, because you feel you show it everyday. If this is your spouse's primary love language, he may not tell you he loves you very often because he feels he shows it by the things he does for you every day.

When this is your gift and not your husband's, you can become very frustrated because you feel that he should "see" things that need done and do them without you having to ask him or tell him. When this emotional need is not met in your life you tend to become critical and demanding as you seek to see things accomplished. Be careful, criticism and demands drive wedges and stop the flow of love. He really doesn't mind if you ask him to do something, he just doesn't naturally see what needs done as you do. Because this is not his primary love language, you will have to ask the next time too!

You must decide daily, that even if he doesn't see things that need to be done, you are going to love him anyway and you are going to try in every way you can to meet his love language. You just might be amazed at what gets done without having to ask!

Love Language #5
Physical Touch

Holding hands, kissing, hugging and sexual intercourse are all ways of communicating emotional love to your spouse. If physical touch is the emotional love language of your spouse than he will require more touches per day than you may require. When you initiate the touching, be it a back rub or running your hand through his hair, you are communicating to him that you love him.

If a person, whose primary emotional love language is physical touch, doesn't receive the needed touches, he withdraws into a shell to avoid hurt. They won't initiate the touching because they feel you should know what their need is. When you take the initiative, they come out of their shell.

When you put forth the effort to learn your spouse's emotional love language and you desire to meet their needs, you are showing sacrificial love. The kind of love that makes marriages last.

So now the question is, where do I begin? Learn your own love language so you can express it to your spouse.

Ask yourself this question: "What hurts me deeply?" (Your response will probably reveal your emotional love language.)

- I hurt most when he makes cutting remarks. (Words of Affirmation)
- I hurt most when he doesn't have time for me. (Quality Time)
- I hurt most when he forgets to buy me a birthday gift. (Receiving Gifts)
- I hurt most when he doesn't see anything that needs to be done. (Acts of Service)
- I hurt most when he doesn't hold my hand in public. (Physical Touch)

Now ask yourself, in what area is your spouse most critical of you? The thing he is the most critical about is probably the area of his life in which you are not meeting his emotional needs. Do you often hear him say:

- You always interrupt me and you're always putting me down. (Words of Affirmation)
- You never want to do anything with me. (Quality Time)
- You never buy me those favorite candies I like. (Receiving Gifts)
- Why isn't his house ever cleaned up? Don't you see what needs done around here? (Acts of Service)
- Why don't you ever sit by me on the couch? (Physical Touch)

Sit down with your spouse and share this information. Discuss how you can best meet each other's emotional love language needs.

When you desire to communicate with someone, you learn his or her language. Make it a point to learn the love language of each of your family members, and speak it frequently!

Chapter Eleven
The Honeymoon Is Over

Adam and Eve were the perfect couple. God had created the latter for the former. Truly a marriage made in heaven. They had perfect communication with God and with each other. They lived peacefully in the most beautiful garden of all creation. They were the perfect couple – but one day they blew it! They lost their paradise because they weren't willing to submit to the King. The Honeymoon was over!

Have you ever wondered how long their honeymoon lasted? No one really knows. It could have been months, years, even hundreds of years, but then something happened. A test came. A trial. Eve was tempted to do something she'd always told herself, "I'll never do that!" Until one day it happened. Certainly that wasn't the first time Satan tempted her, but that day she succumbed.

Marriage is not a Garden of Eden. Problems will come to mess up your paradise! There are rocky times, disappointments, misunderstandings, fights and bleak periods when it seems that even God has abandoned you.

When we get married we falsely expect fair weather and clear sailing. The troubles seem to come first as sprinkles, then in a downpour and eventually as torrential floods! We've got to be prepared. God told Noah to build a boat to save his household from the rains that were going to come. He began working on the boat that would be his salvation, long before he felt that first sprinkle. When the torrents and floods arrived, he felt their impact. The boat rocked and rolled and those inside were probably fearful for their lives. Perhaps they even thought of escaping through that one lone window that God had provided, should they choose to try to make it on their own. But in the end, they were more than glad that they had stayed on the boat.

We have the same options. We can build the spiritual boat in our marriage relationship and get on board to begin the rocking and rolling, or we can take the world's way out by getting a divorce. Jumping ship won't stop the floods from coming; and swimming doesn't cut it in a flood. Divorce is not an option for a Christian. It is a sad commentary, that in the denominal world, the divorce rate is equal to the general population.

In the scheme of life, it does seem that opposites attract. But if we're not careful, when the storms come, the very things that drew us together in the beginning can be the very things that drive us apart. A disorganized person always seems to fall in love with an organized person. Later the disorganization of the one sends the organized one up the wall and the organized one's preciseness drives the other one bonkers! If you got married with the mistaken idea, "When we get married, I'll change him!" Those thoughts could be the beginning of many showers!

You loved him as he was before you were married—don't try to change him now. It only leads to nagging and discontent. Love him unconditionally. If leaving the lid off the toothpaste drives you crazy, buy toothpaste with the flip-top lid that remains attached! Don't rally to jump ship over little idiosyncrasies that don't really matter in eternity! Pray about the situation. Ask God to help you and to give you wisdom. With God's help it is possible to love your spouse into the change that you desire, without your manipulation! And then again, maybe you are the one who needs to change, and God can manage that too!

I was a disorganized, messy housekeeper, but it didn't take me long to realize that when our home was in disarray, my husband was like a fish out of water. He couldn't even think clearly! He didn't nag and was even willing to help clean, but of course that hurt my pride, so I wouldn't allow him to help! I wanted to change but I didn't know how. I prayed that the Lord would help me and found some excellent books to teach me how to get organized and live to tell about it! I could have held out though, being stubborn and refusing to change in an attitude of rebellion. I could have waited until he got to the point that he didn't care how the house looked either, or got fed up with it and left as some men have done.

No matter who we are or where we live, we all have situations that "try" and "test" our marriage to see who and what it is really founded on.

When we first come to God we think we have reached heaven. All our problems will be over! We have that special freshness that comes when we're cleansed and filled with God's Spirit. We have love, joy, peace and fulfillment. But then one day a test comes. We're challenged in our relationship with God. Just as Jesus was tempted in the wilderness to the point that Satan tried to get Him to commit suicide, we will be tempted. When the honeymoon *is* over, we have to decide if we are really committed to the man we married and our relationship, or are we going to silently retreat back into our former existence?

Just as we can't go by "feelings" in our spiritual walk, so it is in our marriage. There may even come a time when you feel you no longer love your spouse. Paul addressed this very issue in Titus 2:4 when he told the aged women to teach the young women to love their husbands. And, "Husbands, love your wives, even as Christ also loved the church, and gave himself for it" (Ephesians 5:25). Satan will make sure you have every opportunity to loose your love for your husband or your wife. That's why it's so important to kindle and rekindle the romance in your marriage.

Just as a butterfly *needs* the physical struggle involved to emerge from his cocoon with strong wing muscles that enable him to fly, we will have struggles to deepen our commitment to the lifelong process of building a relationship in our marriage.

Many men stray because their home-life is mundane. They don't feel appreciated or needed. You can change that! You can make them so excited that they can't wait to get home to see what you've "cooked up" for them—and I don't necessarily mean food!

Thank God for problems. It is through them that we learn to completely trust Him and grow in His image as the Bride of Christ. Look at problems as though they are "homework assignments." If you study hard and pass the test the first time, you may never have to take it again.

By handling our problems with God's principles, we'll receive His promises. It takes a lot of personal discipline, and just plain work, but we *can* do it!

Important marriage principles we need to work on, include the following:

1. **Communication**: Don't clam up. When he asks, "What's wrong?" Don't say, "Nothing!" You'll be telling a lie! Tell him! Ask him to please listen without interrupting and then state your concerns without blaming him, even if you feel he is the one to blame! Sometimes just being able to express your feelings will help you to deal with them in a more positive way. Never go to bed angry. Try to talk things out before you to bed. Go to bed with a positive attitude (Ephesians 4:26).

2. **Compromise**: Learn to give and take. If your immediate reaction to his ideas is "NO," give him a chance! You might find it to be an even better idea than you had. Never forget that God created him to be the head of your family.

3. **Compliment**: Men thrive on compliments from women they love. Make it a point to find something he does well and compliment him for it. Let him know that you appreciate the little things he does as well as the big things. When you make an effort to compliment, you'll find that he will make more of an effort to please you.

4. **Learn**: Don't allow yourself to die mentally or spiritually, keep growing! Learn to communicate without being argumentative. Learn to forgive without holding grudges. Learn to compromise without feeling cheated. Learn to discipline

yourself. Learn something new every day to help you be a better Christian, wife and mother.

5. ***Trust***: What so ever things are true, honest, just, pure, lovely, of good report, if there be any virtue, and if there be any praise, think on these things! Don't think the worst of your husband! Trust him to be the spiritual leader of your home (Philippians 4:8).

6. ***Love***: Above all else, love! Love unconditionally as Christ loves. Build that love relationship into your marriage, don't tear it down. Proverbs is full of wisdom. Do you realize you can pull your home apart with your mouth? David said a nagging wife is like a leaky faucet! We need to dwell on the positive characteristics of one another. Remind yourself daily that your spouse is important to you. God created him and He has a purpose for him that you can help fulfill as his helpmeet!

Actually, it's never too late for a second honeymoon, or third or…

Chapter Twelve

Preparing Children For Life

We were on our way to the airport. Our three children were returning from a month's vacation with Grandma and Grandpa in Ohio and things were going great. We left quite early and had made plans ahead to include a couple of errands on the way to pick them up in San Francisco.

Our first stop was a men's store to pick up a jacket for my husband. We had some extra time, so we tried on a few sale items, then we went next door to the shoe store to see what bargains they had.

The plane was due to arrive at 11:35 a.m. and we still had plenty of time. After all, we'd picked up hundreds of people at the airport, what could possibly go wrong.

We were on the San Mateo Bridge at 10:30, just minutes from the airport, when the traffic came to a dead stop! We sat for a while but we weren't really worried. We still had nearly an hour before their plane touched down. Every few minutes we would move a car length or two, but eventually everything came to a complete halt.

There we sat, and sat, and sat. I definitely began to get anxious. By the time 11:15 rolled around, I was in tears. I knew that the two youngest children would be okay, but I was worried about our oldest. I was afraid she would panic when she realized we weren't there to pick them up. I had been praying, but my prayers became more earnest as it drew closer to their arrival time.

All I could think of was "How could this be happening? Of all the people we've ever picked up at the airport, these are the most important to us! Lord, why this time? Why is this happening to them?"

Cell phones weren't nearly as prolific as they are now and I kept asking my husband to walk ahead to see if he could find a phone to call the airport and tell them what had happened to us. Finally, I convinced him to go in search of a phone in someone's car.

By that time it was after 11:30 and we had seen a plane fly overhead that we were sure was theirs. Worriedly, I began to cry just thinking of them landing and not seeing Mommy or Daddy there—wondering what they would think.

It was beginning to get stuffy in the car and there was nothing I could accomplish by sitting there crying, so I got out to join all the others that were out of their cars enjoying the crisp breeze in an attempt to air their frustrations.

Just as I got out, the man in the car parked beside ours, spoke up, "Boy, I pity anyone who's on the way to the airport to pick someone up!"

I immediately spoke up, "That's us! We're on our way to pick up our children who have been gone for a month and we're sure they've already landed!" I was nearly in tears again.

At that moment, he turned to look me straight in the face, and asked, "Do they know how to pray?"

When he said that, the Lord touched me in the most miraculous way! Instantaneously, He took all my anxiety and fear, and gave me the sweetest peace and comfort!

"Yes," I responded calmly, "They do know how to pray!" In my heart, I rejoiced because I had prepared them for this very situation a long time before it ever happened.

In just a few minutes, my husband sent word back to me that he had found a phone and that the children had landed safely and were with the staff of the airline. He had found a kind man who was willing to drive him all the way to the airport should we get separated from each other in the confusion of the traffic jam.

Traffic finally broke and we arrived at the airport at about 12:30 to find three tired, but excited children. The first thing they said was, "Where were you?" The second thing was, "We weren't scared, we prayed and we knew you were coming!"

What a lesson the Lord impressed upon me that day; the awesome responsibility that we as parents have to teach our children to serve God for themselves.

My husband and I were not raised in the church and our prayer, before we even had children, was "Lord, help us to teach our children to love you and serve you for themselves!"

Unfortunately, we had seen people who were raised in church, but weren't serving God. They were in the church as far as their presence was concerned, but they were apathetic, cynical, rebellious and callous toward real worship, reverence and service to God.

In the scriptures, we are told over and over to teach our children *the faith* diligently, and that we do so by example as well as experience.

"Gather the people together... that their children which have not known anything may hear" (Deuteronomy 31:12-13).

"Come ye children, hearken to me; I will teach you the fear of the Lord" (Psalm 34:11).

"My son, forget not my law, but let thine heart keep my commandments" (Proverbs 3:1).

"And that from a child thou hast known the holy scriptures, which are able to make thee wise unto salvation through faith which is in Christ Jesus" (II Timothy 3:15).

Teach Them To Pray

We need to teach our children how to pray and we should rejoice with them in their answered prayers. Our children have seen over and over, the hand of God as he has met our needs. When we were in Germany, Sharon, our youngest, immensely wanted a bathrobe. We didn't have the extra money to purchase it at the time, so I encouraged her to pray for it. It wasn't long before one of the ladies in our church gave us a huge bag of clothes. Before we even opened it up, I told Sharon that her bathrobe was in it. Sure enough, there was a blue and white terrycloth bathrobe that fit her perfectly! We rejoiced together!

God still hears and answers prayer. He has never changed. He wants to meet our needs whether it is spiritual, emotional, physical or financial. We need to teach our children how to seek God daily in their life.

Teach them to pray in Jesus name. "If ye shall ask any thing in my name, I will do it" (John 14:14). God is still a healer, if you are sick, before you run to the medicine cabinet, have your children pray for you that you will be healed. If your children are sick, place your hand on their forehead and pray that God will touch and heal them, ending the prayer "in Jesus name."

"Is any sick among you? let him call for the elders of the church; and let them pray over him, anointing him with oil in the name of the Lord: And the prayer of faith shall save the sick, and the Lord shall raise him up; and if he have committed sins, they shall be forgiven him" (James 5: 14, 15). Jesus **is** the name of the Lord.

There have been many, many times when we have prayed as a family for particular needs and God has answered in miraculous ways. God's word says that He is no respecter of persons and that He is the same, yesterday, today and forever, so I know that if you go to Him in faith, believing, He will hear and answer your prayers and those of your children.

Build Their Faith

We can teach children to have faith that their prayers will be answered by sharing our own testimony of answered prayers. Many of the miraculous things that have happened in our lives happened before we had children. They have no way of knowing about them unless we take the time to share with them.

Teach them that God is still in the miracle working business. Teach them that He still heals today.

Teach Love

We need to teach our children to love not only others, but themselves as well. We must help our children have a positive self-image.

When our children were little, we used to play a little game around the table that we called "Who loves...?" We would insert one of the names of our family members. Then we would all cheer and get excited about loving that person. One night, my son didn't raise his hand when we called out his name. I asked him why he didn't raise his hand and his response was, "You're not supposed to love yourself." My heart nearly broke. All I could think of was the negative self-image I had grown up with and how hard it was to overcome. I didn't want my son to go through the same struggles.

As a family, we talked about the fact that if you don't love yourself in a proper way, and you were made by God, how could you really love anyone else? The Golden Rule itself is based on the simple fact that you are to love others as you love yourself. "And as ye would that men should do to you, do ye also to them likewise" (Luke 6:31).

These things must be discussed with our children. People who do not love themselves seek to destroy their own body with things in the world that do not satisfy. Satan's goal is to kill, steal and destroy and that is exactly what he is doing to the temples that God created to worship Him as people pierce, cut, tattoo and mutilate their bodies today.

Teach Respect

Respect is not a value replete in our modern society. Radio stations, television and movies are rampant with foul language, lewd remarks and blatant disrespect for anything and everything. Road rage is at epidemic proportions because people have no respect for one another on the highways. Some would rather shoot you than think you cut in front of them and got away with it.

Children need to learn respect for God. He is not "The Man Upstairs," as some people like to refer to Him. He deserves the utmost of honor, reverence and respect. An entire line of clothing based on the term "No fear" touts the lack of awe and reverence of God that is due Him. "The fear of the LORD is the beginning of wisdom..." (Psalms 111:10). Children need to learn to respect the church and how to act in God's house. They need to respect the pastor, to respect his standards and not talk about or berate him. You are not teaching respect to your children when *you* "roast the Pastor for Sunday dinner," by talking about him and criticizing him.

They need to know how to show respect to their parents, teachers, the elderly, guests, other people's property and each other. When children are allowed to hit, punch, and bite their parents, they are being taught the height of disrespect. Teaching children to honor their parents is the first of the Ten Commandments that has a promise with it: "Honour thy father and thy mother: that thy days may be long upon the land which the LORD thy God giveth thee" (Exodus 20:12).

"This know also, that in the last days perilous times shall come. For men shall be lovers of their own selves, covetous, boasters, proud, blasphemers, disobedient to parents, unthankful, unholy, Without natural affection, trucebreakers, false accusers, incontinent, fierce, despisers of those that are good" (II Timothy 3:1-3).

Teach Appreciation

We are such blessed people in our country that we often take things for granted. We want our children to have it better than we did, so we lavish gifts on them that are beyond their age in appropriateness or that overwhelm them in volume. Consequently, they often go unappreciated.

Saying "thank you" does not come naturally, it must be taught. Jesus talked about the fact that in the last days there would be a thankless generation. I have tried very hard to go against that grain. I want to be known as a thankful person and I want my children to know how to say thanks verbally and on paper. Showing appreciation and thankfulness for things people do for you, should be automatic to anyone professing to be a Christian. Even if you don't like the food they fixed for you or the gift they gave you, say thank you and find something to compliment. If someone opens a door for you, thank the person. If they give you a cup of water, thank them.

The best way to teach this to your children is to model it. Let them see you compliment people for things they have done for you. Write thank you notes and teach your children how to write them. Start when they are young even if it is simply drawing a picture to send to the giver.

Teach them to Communicate

Children need to know how to speak to adults and how to introduce people to one another. They need to learn to wait their turn in a conversation and that if they want their parent's attention, to wait for a break in the conversation.

We've all seen the "fits" thrown at the checkout counter by children who think they are going to die if they don't get a candy bar or pack of gum. I've known parents that have succumbed to buying two or three treats to get their child to stop screaming. When you give in, you have lost all sense of discipline in that child's eyes. What you have done is rewarded your child for misbehaving. The child learns that he is the one in control and that he can manipulate you in public. Our rule was, if you asked politely you had a chance of having a treat, if you threw a fit, there were no treats. Children need to learn that there are proper ways of communicating their needs and wants.

Teach Them Discipline

Today *discipline* seems to be a dirty word. Without it, our culture is becoming chaos.

Children need to learn discipline and we need to encourage self-discipline. Allowing your children to drink soda and eat potato chips for breakfast is feeding them a diet that will cause undernourished, sickly bodies. Allowing your children to do what they want when they want will cause undernourished, **sickly** souls.

Teach them the benefits of following the rules by rewarding them. Help them to learn to budget their time and their money. Make **them** pay for superfluous items that are wants rather than needs.

Teach them to discipline their time. I remember walking into my oldest daughter Amy's room one day when she was in junior high, and seeing a list of goals that she wanted to accomplish that particular day. I was really proud of her! She was learning the self-discipline that later helped her to graduate from college with a 4.0 grade point average!

Teach Them To Share Their Faith

Our children need to learn not to be ashamed to share their faith. As Christians, we are compelled to "go into the highways and byways and compel them to come in." Children are not exempt from this heavenly assignment.

Sharing our faith is not teaching the do's and don'ts of the church, but rather the love of Christ and His desire and ability to change our lives.

Teach Them Life Skills

Limit the time they spend playing computer and video games and the time spent watching television and videos. Or, do as many families have done, and eliminate television altogether.

Encourage them to develop a skill or hobby that they enjoy. Encourage them to read.

Don't push them to play a particular instrument or go into your field of work unless they show a sincere interest. Don't be dogmatic, expecting them to do everything to perfection. If they have an interest in the things you do, encourage them in that light. If they like to work on cars or build things but you don't feel particularly qualified in those areas, find someone who can mentor them in that area.

In essence, give them the tools that will enable them to grow in God's ways and equip them to be able to serve God for themselves! It may not be easy but in the end it will be worth it.

I am so thankful that the day my children arrived at the airport and Mom and Dad were nowhere to be found, they knew what to do!

Chapter Thirteen
Blueprints for A Happy Home

Studies have shown that successful homes have several basic rules or guidelines that they try to adhere to. When these "house rules" are understood by all, and followed through with, many problems are eliminated before they arise.

As husbands and wives, we need to be willing to take the necessary steps to learn how to communicate effectively with each other and with our children. Instituting basic principles and guidelines that parents agree on and mutually understand, will help you to have a happy home.

Happy Homes:
Teach Respect for One Another

At home, "company rules" should be the order of the day. Parents must show respect to one another and teach respect to their children.

Children need to be taught manners. We live in a culture where belching and passing gas are laughed at and treated as funny. Children must be taught that these are inappropriate behaviors in public. Yes, they are "facts of life," but they can excuse themselves and go to another room to do them!

Children need to be taught to respect one another's property. They should not take other people's things without permission and they should treat other's possessions with even greater care than their own things.

Children should *never* be permitted to hit or bite their parents. Allowing this behavior is the height of disrespect for parents. I saw one mother whose arms were black and blue with bite marks from her four-year old daughter. She thought she was helping her daughter by allowing her to take out her anger on her mother rather than others. What the mother *was* teaching her daughter was that she was in total control and that it was okay to hurt others to control them. One day, I saw this mother in action at the grocery store. People literally shook their head and scurried to get out of the way as this mother and her two uncontrollable, belligerent, screaming children walked down the aisles.

Happy Homes:
Develop a Sense of Trust

Make it clear in your household, "We do not lie." Satan is the father of lies and we don't want any part of him.

Set the example in your own life. Don't have your child answer the door to an unwanted guest, or answer the phone to an unwanted call and have them say, "I'm sorry but Mommy and Daddy aren't home right now." If you do, you are teaching them to lie.

When you make a promise to your children, you must keep it. If you promise a consequence for inappropriate behavior, keep it.

Let your children know that you mean what you say. Let them know that they can always trust in you and that you want to always be able to trust in them.

Happy Homes:
Have a Sense of Play and Humor

Have fun with your family. If you don't know how to have fun, learn! How can you have a happy home if you don't have fun together?

Make dinner a fun time by sharing the events of the day. Learn to laugh at yourself and be willing to share embarrassing situations with your family so you can all laugh together. My children thought it was hilarious when I told them about standing in line to register for a Teacher Training Workshop. I looked down at my T-shirt top and thought, "Hmmm, I thought this shirt had a pocket in front.... Oh no, this shirt does have a pocket in front!" So I rushed across the huge cafeteria to find a restroom to turn my top around!

Plan simple activities with your children. Play games, make crafts, put puzzles together. Have scavenger hunts, hide their birthday gifts and give them clues as to where to find them. Sing together. Read them stories. Tell them stories from your childhood.

Parents who are serious all the time miss the joys of laughter with their children. I know that with my own children, it was often easier for me to tell my children "no" rather than "yes" when they asked if they could do something. One day I heard a speaker who made the following statement: "When you have a tendency to say "no," stop and ask yourself, "Why do I usually say no? Was what they were asking for actually not good for them, or did I say "no" simply because it was easier on me if I said "no."

Happy Homes:
Exhibit a Sense of Shared Responsibility

Everybody needs to work. Mother is not the hired hand! Even little children can be taught to do simple jobs. They may not be done perfectly, but they need to be taught to do their best in all that they do and that their job is just as important as what everyone else does. Today, with so many working mothers, families need to help more than ever.

I recently read an article about children that were raised in group-home, and foster care settings. At eighteen, when they left the home, they did not have the necessary skills to care for themselves or to make it on their own. They didn't know how to do laundry, grocery shop, cook, manage their money, or look for a job. Research showed that many of these young people were living out of their car or literally on the streets. They had been cared for in the physical sense, but because so many things were ***done for them***, they never learned the life-skills necessary to care for themselves or to make a home run smoothly.

Children need to be taught the proper way to care for themselves, how to shop with an eye for bargains, how to plan meals and cook, how to clean house, how to obtain employment, how to save money, write checks and balance a checkbook, and budget their finances. Home Economics class in Junior High just isn't enough!

Happy Homes:
Teach a Sense of Right and Wrong

It is the ***parent's*** responsibility to teach manners. You do not have to be so rigid that your children are afraid to breathe in your presence, but there are simple rules of respect that need to operate in every home. Those two magic words: Please and Thank-you form the basis of showing respect and appreciation.

Children need to be taught what the family boundaries are, what things are permissible and what things are just not acceptable. When our children were young, we had a rule that if they wanted a friend to come over, they needed to respect us enough to ask us in private. If they forgot, and asked in front of the friend, the answer was an automatic "no." Some things just need to be discussed in private.

Gary Smalley refers to this as a Family Constitution. When you decide as a family what the rules are and what the consequences are if a rule is broken, then parents aren't seen as the "bad guys." The rules are the rules. The offenders, be they children or parents, face the consequences when they break the rules.

Discuss with your children how you expect them to act in public. Tell them what the rewards for good behavior will be and what the consequences for bad behavior will be and then follow through with your promises. Parents often do not realize that not following through with these promises, whether negative or positive, is actually lying to your child. If your children know that what you are saying is idle threats, they will take total advantage of you in public. Follow through is of the utmost importance.

Let's face it, kids who have manners are liked! Kids who are belligerent to parents, demanding, and rude are an insult to themselves and to their parents. We are admonished in scripture to, "Correct thy son, and he shall give thee rest; yea, he shall give delight unto thy soul" (Proverbs 29:17).

Happy Homes:
Value Service to Others

It is important to teach our children that we are givers, not takers. We need to show them by example that we don't have to get paid for everything we do for others. Teach them that it is important to help the elderly and disabled shovel snow from their sidewalk, rake their leaves and to carry their groceries. His word teachers us that we are to minister to the elderly, widows, orphans and the poor, expecting nothing in return. We need to teach our children that when we give to others, God will repay us, He will bless us in return. His word teaches that when we do kind things in secret, He will reward us openly.

I love the little books that have recently been published entitled *Random Acts of Kindness*. They tell of hundreds of ways that we can bless others in simple every day things that take very little effort, just a little thoughtfulness.

Also teach your children to follow Biblical principles in giving at church. Teach them how to tithe and the blessing of giving to missions and other special offerings. Share with them times you have given sacrificially and how God has blessed you as a result. Tell them of times when you have had a need that God used someone else to fill. Let them see you be a cheerful giver. "Every man according as he purposeth in his heart, so let him give; not grudgingly, or of necessity; for God loveth a cheerful giver" (II Corinthians 9:7).

Happy Homes:
Share a Religious Core Value System

Children need to be taught that God is real and that there is an eternal judgement that we will all face one day. In the "old days," they used to say, "There's a heaven to gain and a hell to shun!" The same is true today.

Children need to be taught that there is one God and that His name is Jesus. It is the parent's responsibility to teach their children about God. "Hear, O Israel: The LORD our God is one LORD: And thou shalt love the LORD they God with all thine heart, and with all thy soul, and with all thy might. And these words, which I command thee this day, shall be in thine heart: And thou shalt teach them diligently unto thy children, and shalt talk of them when thou sittest in thine house, and when thou walkest by the way, and when thou liest down, and when thou risest up" (Deuteronomy 6: 4-7).

Children need to be taught that sometimes life is not fair. Scripture tells us that the rain falls on the just and the unjust, but that God is always just. We can't explain why tragedies happen other than the fact that there is sin in the world, but we can teach them that God is preparing a place for those that serve Him where there is no sin, or pain or heartache.

Children need to be taught that there are "absolutes." Some things are always right and some things are always wrong. They need to know that there are moral laws that must not be broken, glossed over, or compromised.

Children need to be taught how to pray, how to read and memorize scripture and how to apply scripture to their own lives. They need to be taught that God doesn't have any grandchildren, He only has children. We are not saved because we walk in the religious traditions of our parents. We are saved when we have a personal relationship with God. We must serve God for ourselves!

Happy Homes:
Respect the Privacy of One Another

Children need to be taught that before opening a closed door, they need to knock politely and *wait for a response* before entering. Parents also need to give their children the same respect in this matter.

Modesty is still a virtue that needs to be taught. Family members should always be dressed decently in front of one another, especially in these days of "blended" families.

Children should not be sleeping with their parents. The simple practice of allowing a nursing newborn to sleep with you because it's just more convenient, turns into a nightmare very quickly when you try to get them to sleep in their own bed at a later date. This is not a good practice for the intimacy of a husband and wife, and it is not a good precedent for the child's maturity. If this is already a problem, take a stand and do not allow them to sleep with you any longer. If this has gone on for some time, it may take one or two nights of loud protests, but if you are persistent, you will all be better off in the days to come.

We live in a day and age when nearly fifty percent of all women and twenty-five percent of all men, have been abused sexually at some point in their life. Often times, this abuse has occurred when, as children, they spent the night at someone's house. I would like to caution you *not to allow* your children to stay overnight at other people's houses. If you have company in your home, don't allow the children to sleep together. I know this sounds harsh, but you never know what other children have been exposed to in the media and/or at the hand of some perpetrator. As the old adage goes, "better safe than sorry."

From an early age, teach your children that as a family, you have no secrets. If someone tells your child "don't tell anyone what happened," that child needs to know that he or she can tell you because in your home there are no secrets.

Teach your children "good touch, bad touch." If someone touches them in an area where they feel uncomfortable, they need to feel free to tell you what happened.

I personally know of four ministerial families that were affected by abuse as a result of spending a night with a "friend." It is just not worth the risk.

Happy Homes:
Admit the need for and seek help with problems

When problems arise in a family that cannot be solved by traditional means, seek outside help. Talk with your pastor, make an appointment with your family physician, or contact a highly recommended Christian Counselor, but get help.

Some warning signs of serious problems are prolonged depression, personality changes, seclusion, secretive and withdrawn behavior and severe weight loss or gain. Seek professional help as quickly as possible if you see these signs in your loved ones.

These are the 'last days' and there are spiritual forces that are bombarding Christians like never before. Don't allow your family to fall victim to their prey, seek help as quickly as possible.

God truly wants our home to be the happiest place on earth, but it doesn't happen without our time, effort and commitment! Seek God daily as you diligently make your home happy and successful with God's blueprints.

Chapter Fourteen
Blessing Your Children

Throughout scripture, we see tangible examples of parents passing on "the blessing" to their children. The first blessing we see in the Bible, is God as he blessed Adam, his son, in the Garden of Eden. In Genesis 49:28 we see Jacob blessing his twelve sons, "And this is it that their father spake unto them, and blessed them; every one according to his blessing he blessed them."

Sometimes as parents, we are so involved in the "caring for" or the maintenance aspect of raising our children, that we fail to take the time to truly bless them. This chapter is designed to help you think of many wonderful ways that you can bless your children on a daily basis.

When we bless our children, we share with them the heritage of our past and give them hope for the future. We share with them, through example, the blessing of the Lord and how He has helped us each and every day. When we bless our children, we build a hedge of protection about them.

Children, today, need to know the love of their parents is strong. Kids who don't feel their parents love and blessing do not feel accountable to them. They take their problems to other parents, school counselors or even street gangs where they feel loved, appreciated and accepted.

We live in a generation "where the love of many has waxed cold" (Matthew 24:12). I call it "The Generation of Throw Away Children." Parents are not only killing their pre-born children; they are also killing those several years old! Children, who are a burden to their parent's lifestyle, are given to grandparents, neighbors and institutions to be raised. In the stores and on the street we hear parents cursing their children with hideous vulgarities and threats. Is it any wonder we see such rebellion today?

We can't afford not to show added kindness to our children, because their lives will touch the lives of those whose parents really don't care. If our children don't feel our total love and support, they will be drawn away into the world's culture because there, in a very warped way, they *will* feel loved and appreciated.

When we "bless" our children, we connect with their heart. They know that they are very special and important to us. Giving your continual blessing through love, respect and strong, consistent, fair discipline is the key.

Most parents are better lecturers than they are listeners, yet listening to children is crucial in developing their self-esteem and sense of belonging. When adults take time to listen to a child, that child feels that what they have to say is important. They realize that what they think, holds value. Children must feel that they are valuable to their parents and to the total family structure.

Developing a "sense of family" is extremely important. Rituals and traditions say: I love you, I like being with you, and I want to re-in-act what is important in life with you because you are important to me. Family traditions help bring stability to families that move frequently.

We lived in Germany as missionaries when our children were young. Our children were uprooted from both family and friends and taken to a new land and culture. Knowing how many things had changed in their lives, I felt, for their stability, it was important to keep as many things as possible, the same so I tried to keep as many family traditions as I could. We had always celebrated Christmas by having a decorated tree. Our first year there, we were unable to have one, so I made each child a four foot tall, red velvet stocking, to take the place of the missing tree. The children loved them and the tree was almost forgotten! Our Christmas Eve tradition of sitting as a family while one of the children read the Christmas Story, then going around the circle to tell each other our blessings and what we are thankful for, remained in tact, as it has to this day. (Even though our children are adults now, they still seem to forget whose turn it is to read the Christmas Story! They all want the honor!)

Sharing your own childhood with your children, helps them to understand who you are. That you really were a child at one time in your life is hard for some children to comprehend. Take your children to the house you lived in when you were born and show them the area where you grew up. Drive by the schools you attended and mention what was important to you when you went there. Tell them about your favorite teachers, field trips and experiences as you remember them. Tell them about the autumn pastel picture you drew in the forth grade that was hung in the front hall for all to see at Open House. Tell them how special that clay piece was that you sculpted and the art teacher fired for you for your Mother's Day project!

Take them to the parks you played in as a child. Let them roll down the same grassy hill you rolled down in the summer and sledded down in the winter. Walk with them on the same wooded paths you walked as a child. Point out the tree that you always thought looked like a deer with antlers. Share with them how you played hide and seek or cowboys and Indians... or simply how you collected leaves for your science notebook. Build as many memories as you can!

They may be interested in your first job, where it was, what you did, and of course how little money you made!

Sharing your past with your children gives them a sense of identity. It helps them to know you as a person. Many parents have very humble beginnings and explaining this to your child helps them to have a much better perspective on why your values and motives are as they are. It helps them to relate to the fact that you really were a baby once. That you had to grow up, just as they are, and that you had tests and trials just as they do.

Keeping a journal or notebook of things that your children do or say, is precious and priceless. So many things happen and are said daily, that our mind soon forgets what we thought we would never forget. Getting the incident down on paper keeps it ever fresh, ready to share or relive at any moment. Children love to hear you tell stories about things they did when they were little.

If your children are older and you never thought to keep a record of some of the cute things they did and said, it's still not too late. Take some time, get a pencil and some paper and ask God to refresh your memory. As you reminiscence, you'll be surprised how many things will creep back to your memory. They may not be exactly true to form, but they will be special blessings from the past to share with your child.

When our children were teens, I presented each of them with a mini-biography. I began with the day they were born with all the little details, and went on to tell individual family reactions to their special birth. I wrote about their likes and dislikes, favorite toys, things they did and said, special places they went, friends they had when they were too little to remember, early babysitters... I tried to think of as many things as I could that they probably wouldn't otherwise remember. They loved their personalized biography.

If you have moved frequently, you may want to take them to see where they were born and where they lived as a newborn. Show them the first restaurant in which they created a scene! Remind them of the time they pitched french-fries backwards over their shoulder and you embarrassingly saw one glide across a neighboring table!

If your children are still quite small, make a photo album of family members they don't get to see very often. Talk about your family members and they will look forward to seeing Grandma and Grandpa rather than being frightened of them.

Plan special outings with each child. Make a date to have lunch with them. Pick them up from school and take them to a favorite fast food restaurant. If there isn't anyplace to go nearby, go to a park with a picnic lunch or take them home for a specially prepared treat. If you work during the day and are unable to take them to lunch, then plan to do so on Saturday afternoon. If you can't afford to go out to eat, perhaps you could pick one day a month and cook each child's favorite meal. Make sure that you reiterate to your child that you've made his or her favorite meal because they are so special to you. Some families have a "plate of honor" that is used on special occasions to make the person whose event they are celebrating, feel extra special.

Allow their friends to come to your house to play. When they are at your house, you set the rules and you can monitor their behavior. You don't have to worry about where they are and what they are doing. You are also setting the stage for later years. When your children know that their friends like you, and enjoy being with you, they won't mind you chaperoning their events. And they will enjoy "hanging out" at your house rather than cruising the square.

Plan a date with an older child. Take them to a special restaurant that requires them to dress nicely. This is especially nice for fathers of teenage girls.

We did something very special for each of our children when they turned sixteen. My husband took them on a date. They went to a very nice restaurant for dinner and he presented them with a covenant gift. We gave a birthstone ring to each of our daughters and our son received a beautiful watch. This covenant gift was a promise between father and teen, that they would keep themselves pure until the day they married. When our oldest daughter married, during the ceremony, my husband asked for her to return the ring that he had given her when she turned sixteen. He then gave the ring to her husband as a token of the fact that he was marrying a girl that had kept herself clean and pure in the sight of God. She was a woman who had chosen to save herself for her husband! As you can imagine, this was a very special moment for all of us.

We tried to think of something special to do for our children when they had exceptionally good report cards. We didn't "pay" them for grades but we would treat them with something they had been wanting or a family day out.

Keeping a scrapbook for your child requires extra diligence on your part but what a special way to bless your child! Many families put together a special album to present to their young person at graduation or as a wedding keepsake. I kept a folder for each child in which I deposited personal notes I received from them. When they were younger I saved their school papers after they were removed from the refrigerator display. I also saved special art projects and hope to get one or two of them framed as time goes on. Do make sure you write the date on the item and the child's name. You think you will never forget who made you that special card, but in time you will. My son is twenty-one and I still have the certificate stating that he knows his color words!

In our family, we write notes to one another. Sometimes we leave them on the table, on a pillow, in a book or in a lunch bag. Putting a little note in your child's lunch bag that simply says, "I love you," may be exactly what they need to get them through the remainder of the day! My children always seemed to remember to tell me thanks for the note, with an extra hug attached when they got home from school or work. Sometimes I wrote notes on the outside of their lunch bag to bless their friends a little too!

Our son went through a rough time a year or so ago. He had a broken leg and a broken ankle and for three months, was extremely dependent on Mom and Dad for everything. When he was finally able to get back to work, he was still feeling down, so even at his age, I tried to think of something to cheer him up a little. I came across some stickers that were really cute: Bug Sandwich, Beware of this lunch, This lunch was packed especially for you by your Mom... just silly little stickers to bring a smile. Whenever I would put one of them in his lunch, he would respond with a note to me. It was just light enough to get him to smile and encourage him through the rest of the day.

Kids love *Post It* notes because they stick to almost anything. Invest in a little pack and post your love for them all over the house, on cereal boxes, mirrors, shoes, etc! They also love to receive mail. Don't wait until you are gone on a trip without them to send a card, postcard or note. Send a note "just because." Send for freebies in their name. Many publications offer free posters, books and stickers for merely sending them your name and address. The library has books for kids that list hundreds of free and inexpensive things to send for. Surprise them with a magazine subscription that they will receive and enjoy all year.

Daily mealtime is very important. If at all possible, try to have at least one meal a day as a family unit. This is a time for laughter, for sharing, and for teaching manners. It is a bonding time as you sit together at the end of the day to take time enjoying fellowship. Sunday mornings were sometimes difficult to get everyone up to get ready for church, so we started a tradition many years ago that we call "Big Breakfast." I make homemade biscuits, which we eat with maple syrup and we have cheese eggs and breakfast meat if I have it on hand. The biscuits might be round or they might be hearts or stars, depending on the season. Even as adults, it is much easier to get everyone up in good humor when we have "Big Breakfast!" I think, that even more than breakfast, they enjoy the tradition.

Children love to write with chalk on the sidewalk. What would they think if you wrote them a love note on the sidewalk! I never understood why drawing with chalk on the sidewalk was such a no-no. It washes right off! In Europe many aspiring artists draw magnificent drawings on the downtown sidewalks. As the admiring pedestrians walk by, they drop coins into a hat or cup. No one is shooed away and everyone sidesteps the masterpiece until nature decides to wipe the slate clean. Perhaps you could encourage your budding artist to indulge by presenting them with their own pack of colored sidewalk chalks.

Decorate your child's door with a name sign and something that they like. Make their room a pleasant place to be. Paint it if you need to. Perhaps you could add a touch of wallpaper or border. Don't allow them to deface the walls. Show them where crayons and markers can be used appropriately. Teach them to respect the home your family shares. A room that is nice looking is more fun to be in and easier to tidy up. Teach them how to make their bed and organize their things. If they know where you want them to put things, they are more likely to get there! Sleep in their bed sometime to see if it is comfortable.

Bedtime stories are always welcomed. Whether you make them up as you go, or read from a treasured book. The special time of sharing will help your child to relax and you will be fulfilling a vital need in their young lives. Research shows that the more children are read to, the better readers they end up becoming. The sound of words and the rhythm of language is taught as you read to children on a consistent basis. Simple books that they memorize and "read" with you, also aid in the process of learning to read.

Tuck your children in bed and pray with them as long as they will allow you to. As young teens, I still enjoyed tucking our children into bed. My son would roll from side to side, forming his mummy cocoon as he snuggled in for the night. Our house sounded like "The Walton's" as we lay in bed and said our goodnights!

Here are some quick ideas to help your child feel your blessing:
- Make a banner or pennant for your child out of fabric, felt or even a computer printout. Banners and pennants advertise how special you are!
- Hang a string of hearts over their doorway.
- Fill a closet with balloons, just for the fun of it!
- Make statements that bless: "I like the way you…" "I love you because…" "You're special because…."

- Have your child pick a number from one to ten, then give them that number of kisses.
- Have a secret code that allows you to tell your child that you love them without saying any words. Three quick hand squeezes expresses "I love you" quite well.
- Pick a special nickname for your child. A name that attaches a special quality to their life, example: Sharing Sharon.
- Make a "love collage" for your child, or with his help. Include their name, initials, letters they've written, pictures and items of special interest to them.
- Give your child a framed family picture. It keeps the importance of the family ever present, and reminds them of their special place in the family.
- Children often pick flowers for their parents or give them as gifts, how about you giving them fresh flowers for their room!
- Serve your child breakfast in bed, or lunch on the patio with your presence.
- If you're going on a trip or you have a fairly long commute to church, take a book to read along the way. You can do all the reading or family members can take turns reading to one another. Everyone enjoys it and it makes the drive seem shorter.
- Relieve them of a chore for a day.
- Pick up the clothes in their room one day, without complaining about it!
- Start a collection for them. Our children each get a new ornament for Christmas. When they leave home to begin their own family, they take a part of the "family tree" with them.
- Help them to pursue a hobby. Get involved in a hobby with them. Children really open up when you work with them side by side in a non-threatening situation.

- Make a recipe book for them that includes their favorites plus other staple recipes they will need some day.
- Let them use your kitchen, tools, machines, etc. Lay down the ground rules on how they must be cared for, used, cleaned and replaced. Revoke the privilege for a time if they abuse it. In doing so, you are teaching responsibility and caring for the property of others.
- As they leave the house each day, let them leave with your blessing not your scolding! Have things as organized as possible so that when they leave in the morning it is with pleasant thoughts and a desire to return to their safe haven as soon as possible! You could have a basket or box near the door and as things are readied for school, have them put their things in the basket so they can grab it on their way out.

Basically, what I am saying, is take the time to raise your children with purpose, praise, and the power of God. Let them know that just as their heavenly father loves them unconditionally, you do too! Give them your blessing every day both verbally and in the way you respond to them. Eternity will reap the benefits one way or the other.

Chapter Fifteen

Prayer Makes the Difference

A.J. and Thomas are two boys in our Sunday school program. Thomas was learning to read in school and was considerably taller than A.J. In Sunday school we sing a song that simply says: "Read your Bible, pray every day and you'll grow, grow, grow... Don't read your Bible, don't pray every day and you'll shrink, shrink, shrink...." One day A.J. asked his mother, "Mom, I talk to Jesus every day, but I can't read yet, is that why Thomas is taller than I am?" Oh that we would take things as literally as children do!

It is true, if we want to grow spiritually; we must have daily communion with God. We communicate with God by praying and by reading His word. Three problems hinder spiritual growth in prayer and spiritual growth in understanding God's word:

- Having a heart with unforgiveness
- Not knowing how to pray
- Not developing the discipline to pray

Just as we desire communication and relationship with those we love, God desires the same with us. We are His children. He desires to instruct us in the "way we should go," but we must make ourselves available to Him.

Through the years, I have desired to have a deeper relationship with God. I've read numerous books on prayer and how to study the Bible. When I'm not careful, I find myself spending more time reading books on prayer and Bible study, than I do actually praying and reading the Bible! Reading books *can* help us *only if* we put their suggestions into practice!

The best way to learn how to pray is by praying. Thee best way to learn God's word is by studying and reading it!

Today's lifestyles are so busy that unless we purposefully schedule time for God into our day, more than likely, we will probably never have the necessary time. Determine in your heart that you will make the time. That it will become an integral part of your daily routine.

The best time for me to pray and study is early in the morning. I get up an hour earlier than I need to. In the morning I am more refreshed and alert, plus everyone else is still sleeping, so it is quiet. Your best time might be in the afternoon when your little ones are napping, or perhaps you can have lunch with the Lord each day. If you are a night person, then meet with the Lord each evening at a designated time.

Larry Lea's book, ***Could You Not Tarry One Hour?*** gives an excellent pattern to follow in daily devotional prayer. In his teaching on prayer, Lea says, "As I obeyed the call to pray, the Holy Spirit revealed secrets of prayer. I learned how to worship the Lord and to make powerful faith declarations based upon His names and promises. I learned how to pray in God's provision… how to pray a hedge of protection about myself, my family and my possessions, and how to stand in the victory Jesus has won for me.

God wants to speak to you, but you need the vehicle of prayer, for God does not reveal Himself to casual inquirers."

Lea believes that what we have traditionally called the Lord's Prayer is actually a model prayer in which Jesus outlines six topics as a pattern to be followed under the guidance of the Holy Spirit. He says that these six topics should be included in our daily prayer time, for they cover all our needs. Lea uses a prayer outline based upon the Lord's prayer as found in Matthew 6:9-13. This is a brief outline of Lea's teaching on prayer:

Our Father which art in heaven, Hallowed be thy name. We need to begin prayer with honor and praise to God. We need to honor and worship His name.

Thy Kingdom come. Thy will be done. Tell God that you desire His will and priorities to be established in yourself, your family, your church and your nation. Pray over each of these items, one by one.

Give us this day our daily bread. God desires to meet your daily needs, but you must be specific. Don't pray in generalities.

Forgive us our debts as we forgive our debtors. Ask God to help you have right attitudes with others regardless of what you feel they have done to hurt you. You must forgive and release others if you want God to forgive you and remove your sin.

And lead us not into temptation but deliver us from evil. Daily pray a hedge of protection around yourself, your loved ones, your home, and your finances. You should also put on the whole armor of God as outlined in Ephesians 6:14-17.

For thine is the kingdom, and the power, and the glory for ever. Amen Again we need to praise God, not just for the things He does for us, but because of who He is. He is our Lord, our Saviour, the most Holy One. He is the lifter of our soul. He is the great Shepherd. He is the Alpha and Omega, the beginning and the end. Jesus is everything!

I can't emphasize enough the power of forgiveness to release us to have power with God in prayer. "If I regard iniquity in my heart, the Lord will not hear me" (Psalms 66:18). "Confess your faults one to another, and pray one for another, that ye may be healed. The effectual fervent prayer of a righteous man availeth much" (James 5:16).

David said, "Search me O Lord, know my heart. See if there be any wicked way in me." If we have a superior attitude concerning spiritual things, if we have divided motives or pride, our prayers will be hindered. "For the eyes of the Lord are over the righteous, and his ears are open unto their prayers: but the face of the Lord Is against them that do evil" (I Peter 3:12). "To whom ye forgive any thing, I forgive also: for if I forgave any thing, to whom I forgave it, for your sakes forgave I it in the person of Christ; Lest Satan should get an advantage of us: for we are not ignorant of his devices" (II Corinthians 2:10). When we do not forgive those who have tresspassed against us, Satan has an advantage over us, in essence he is controlling us, or hindering us in our relationship to God because he still has a stronghold in our life.

There are many "formulas" designed to help you pray, but the important thing is to pray! I have recently found a simple way to keep myself on task when I pray. I write my prayer requests and scriptures to pray on spiral bound 3X5 cards. I have each section of the Lord's prayer on a separate card and specific things to pray regarding that topic. When I find scriptures to pray that meet needs or situations that I'm praying about, I jot them down on a card. As I pray, I pray through each card. I'm usually not able to get through them all on a daily basis. Sometimes I only get to one or two cards because God takes over in intercessory prayer. As I pray, I flip each card to the back. The next day I simply begin where I left off. Each day's prayers have become unique and refreshing. I no longer fight sleep or run out of things to pray about.

All too often, prayer is us talking to God. One author said, "Prayer is not an intercom system that calls God as if He is a Butler to do our bidding. But rather, prayer is like a walkie-talkie in the midst of the battle, awaiting orders from the commander in chief!" We need to allow the Holy Spirit to take control and direct our thoughts as we pray. Praying in the spirit, intercessory prayer, moves spiritual mountains we cannot see in the natural realm. "Likewise the Spirit also helpeth our infirmities: for we know not what we should pray for as we ought: but the Spirit itself maketh intercession for us with groanings which cannot be uttered. And he that searcheth the hearts knoweth what is the mind of the Spirit, because he maketh intercession for the saints according to the will of God. And we know that all things work together for good to them that love God, to them who are the called according to his purpose" (Romans 8:26-28).

Keeping a prayer journal is very helpful in times of stress. I have gone through periods in my life where I have written letters to God. As He answered and spoke to my heart, I wrote His words down. Jotting down dated prayer requests and their answers are a wonderful encouragement. It truly helps us to realize "how right on time" our God is! Be careful to give God praise and thanksgiving as he answers your prayers.

It is extremely important that we pray "according to God's will." And this is the confidence that we have in him, that, if we ask any thing according to his will, he heareth us: And if we know that he hear us, whatsoever we ask, we know that we have the petitions that we desired of him. (1 John 5:14-15) Praying in God's will isn't easy, but it puts you in complete oneness with the will of God.

Too often we only see what we want to happen so we pray "our will be done" without realizing we are taking it out of "God's will" at that point. We must come to the point where we can pray: "Lord, not my will, but Thine be done. No matter how much it hurts, how difficult the task may be, how high the mountain you've given me to climb, it doesn't make any difference, dear Lord, I am willing."

When you pray God's perfect will, He opens doors and fantastic things begin to happen as a result of making ourselves totally available to Him. When God opens a door we need to be willing to accept His leadership, knowing He will give us the strength and grace to go through it. We need to pray that God will lead us through whatever doors He has for us.

Don't pray answers, pray requests. When people ask you to pray that such and such will happen, kindly tell them, "I do not pray answers, I pray requests!" When we pray answers, we are demanding that God do something just the way we want it done. When we bring the need to God and pray according to His will, we give Him free reign to do as He sees best, which we know is so much higher than we can ever ask or think.

"Pray without ceasing" (I Thessalonians 5:17). "Men (& women) ought always to pray" (Luke 18:1). Keep yourself open to God at all times. Regardless of what you are doing, when you think of something that needs prayer, pray! I have heard of hundreds of situations where people have felt impressed to pray for someone, having no idea what might be happening or even who the person was, but when dates and times were compared, it was the exact time that prayer was needed to bring about God's perfect will in the situation.

One story I will never forget was of a Pastor's wife who was washing her dishes. God gave her a vision of a man in a bamboo cage and she literally fell to her knees in prayer and travail for this man. When the burden lifted, she finished doing her dishes. Years later she was at some sort of meeting and she saw the very man that was in her vision. Talking with him confirmed the fact that he had indeed been in a bamboo cage and it was at the time of her prayers that a critical decision was being made as to his release!

Nona Freeman, veteran missionary to Africa, shared the story that many years ago in Arkansas she too was doing household chores when God spoke to her to go out on the front porch and wave a dish towel towards the road. She did as the Lord told her. She stood out there and waved the towel for several minutes, not really understanding why, when finally a car came down the road and passed by her house. When she saw the car she began waving enthusiastically. The man in the car acknowledged the wave but drove on. She stood a few minutes more then she went back into the house. She told the Lord, "Well I don't know what that was all about but I did what you told me to do!" Years later, when they were raising funds to return to Africa, they were in a church in their hometown. A man shared his testimony of how he was on his way out of town to kill himself, thinking no one cared about him, when Nona, the Pentecostal Preacher's wife, stood on her front porch waving enthusiastically at him as he drove by. The thought that someone really did care about him, kept him from committing suicide and he later gave his heart to God.

Both of these incidents took place because women were willing to pray without ceasing and obey the voice of God.

Each day as we pray, we should ask God what we should pray for. We should ask him what he would have us do for the day. We should ask if there is someone that He would like us to call or stop to see. We think we should plan our day and then pray, when what we should do is pray, then allow God to help us plan our day.

SOS prayers are those we pray on the spot. Perhaps you see an accident, pray for the victims and the caregivers. You get a distressing phone call, you pray with the person on the phone or as soon as you hang up. You are talking with someone and they mention a particular physical need, be bold enough to ask if you can pray for them right there. Some will tell you "no," others will say "yes." What a testimony of God's power when they immediately feel His healing hand in their situation. I truly believe that in these last days, we are going to see more and more miracles, and as a result, they are going to draw people to Christ. We have had people come to our church because their Pastor told them that he didn't personally believe in healing today. We have Pastors and church elders in our town directing people to our services to receive prayer for healing!

"We need to pray for those things which be not, as though they were" (Romans 4:17). When we first moved to Monroe, (our current church) as a church body, we began to pray for all of the people that would eventually fill the empty pews. Today, the pews are full to overflowing and we are in a building program! Last year we spent one night a month, snow, sunshine or rain, walking and praying through our town, asking God to set the captives free, and to deliver people from drugs, alcohol and other perversions. We asked God to open the spiritual eyes of people who were hungry to know Him in truth and to break the bonds of traditional religion. Within the last two months, we have had three men come to the Lord who not only had been doing drugs, but were also dealing drugs! God is *still* in the prayer answering business! We just have to take Him at His word. If my people, which are called by my name, shall humble themselves, and pray, and seek my face, and turn from their wicked ways; then will I hear from heaven, and will forgive their sin, and will heal their land. Now mine eyes shall be open, and mine ears attend unto the prayer that is made in this place. 2 Chronicles 7: 14 & 15

God will answer your prayers, but you have to pray them first! Generic prayers are not what He is seeking. He desires genuine, heartfelt prayers that seek His perfect will.

Begin today to seek His face. Seek the LORD, and his strength: seek his face evermore. Psalms 105:4 What this means is that we are to worship Him. So often when we pray, we are asking for things. As God, He desires that we seek Him to worship Him. This is really what prayer is all about, the act of communicating with God in an intimate way that shows Him we love Him for who He is, not just for the things He does for us.

Chapter Sixteen
Study to Show Yourself Approved

During a recent conversation with some friends, the old saying, "Cleanliness is next to Godliness," was quoted. One person spoke up and said, "Well, you know that is in the Bible!" Several people concurred and some discussion ensued before I spoke up and said, "No it isn't! That's just an old saying that people think is in the Bible!"

My friend was shocked! She was sure she had heard her Pastor make that statement from the pulpit and credit it to the Bible! I told her that if she ever found it in the scriptures I would appreciate knowing where it was!

One day, in a conversation with a friend about modern lifestyles, I mentioned that the Bible said that in the last days it would be like Sodom and Gomorrah. My friend said that she had never been taught anything about Sodom and Gomorrah or its relationship to homosexuality, even though she had been "confirmed" in her denominational church.

In literature, when Bible characters are mentioned, it is assumed that people will know who they are talking about. Today's students don't have a clue who David is, or Moses, or Jonah. Unfortunately, even people who have received religious instruction from their churches, have no idea that the Bible is relevant today, that it literally is the Living Word of God and that even the common man can understand it.

A recent statistic stated that we now have the most educated generation that the United States has ever known. Unfortunately, we probably also have the most Biblically illiterate generation our nation has ever known. Few people really know what God's word says. People who do go to church, allow someone else to read and interpret the scripture for them. They do nothing of their own volition to know and understand it, accepting as fact what someone else tells them.

Contrary to popular belief, the Bible is not a difficult book to understand. Political and Spiritual leaders have made it appear to be complicated and confusing to enable them to maintain control of the masses. Church teachings by certain organizations around 325 AD stated that only the priests were able to accurately interpret the scriptures. Bibles were literally chained to the pulpits during the Dark Ages because the ruling church, at that time, did not want the common man to have access to God's word. A man by the name of Guttenberg felt so strongly that the Bible needed to be in the hands of the common man, that he developed the printing press to mass-produce the scriptures. He was considered a heretic and paid for this crime with his very life.

God desires that we be students of His word! What a privilege to have the freedom and ability to read and study God's word for ourselves. His Word will not waiver and it will not return to us void. When we read it for ourselves, we can know who God is and who we are in God. Let us never neglect this responsibility, relegate it to others, or take it for granted!

"Search the scriptures; for in them ye think ye have eternal life: and they are they which testify of me" (John 5:39).

"Study to show thyself approved unto God, a workman that needeth not to be ashamed, rightly dividing the word of truth" (II Timothy 2:15).

There are many ways to read and study the Bible. I would like to introduce you to some basic tools, general principles and "how to's" that will help you to get the most from your Bible reading efforts.

Keys to Effective Bible Study

Some people use the "hunt and peck" system of Bible Reading. They only read scriptures that pertain to a subject of interest to them. Some merely open their Bible randomly, asking God to direct them to a daily scripture passage. These methods will in no way feed you the word of God as it is intended to do so.

The most important keys to effective Bible study are having a system and consistency. Making a commitment to yourself and to God is crucial whether you want to read the Bible from cover to cover or you want to research a particular person or event.

Systematic reading gives you a balanced view of God. When you read the Bible at random, you tend to pick out parts you are familiar with, you don't open yourself up to learning more, and you miss the total picture. For serious Bible study, it is good to read the entire Bible through at least once and then go back and study individual books more closely.

You may want to study a particular book or series of books such as the Gospels, the Major Prophets, or Poetry. You may want to study a particular theme throughout the Bible, such as: love, peace, obedience....

Don't just read it once, read it repeatedly. The Bible is unlike any other book written. It is a living document! It holds new and deeper meaning each time you read it because as you grow spiritually, new light and understanding is opened up to you. Something you feel you may have read hundreds of times, will suddenly hold truths that you never saw before!

Basic Tools for Study

The first thing you need is a good Study Bible. Today there are many different translations and paraphrases available. Please keep in mind, that not all translations are accurate. I prefer the King James Version for daily reading, memorization and study. I also like to use the *Amplified Bible* because it is easy to read and it "amplifies" or further explains the meaning of the words in the text.

There are many "specialty" Bibles that target certain groups of individuals: *Men's Devotional Bible, Women's Devotional, The One Year Bible, The Spirit-Filled Bible...* Do be careful, many Bibles are printed with added text or commentaries that tend to draw your mind away from the actual scriptures. Their interpretation or explanation of the scriptures may be misleading. A Study Bible, such as *The Thompson-Chain Reference Bible*, published by the Kirkbride Company, is an excellent study Bible. It gives no scriptural commentary written by man, but it has literally thousands of references that lead you through the scriptures as you study particular subjects, ideas and people.

The next thing you need is a notebook. As you read and study God's word, new revelations and understandings will come to you. Keep track of these thoughts in a notebook.

You may even want to keep a Spiritual Journal (as mentioned in another chapter) that reflects your spiritual growth as you read and study God's word. After you read a passage of scripture, you can record how it related to you, how you felt about it, what you learned about it and any new questions that you have. At the end of this chapter, you will find sample formats or worksheets that you can use to help you keep a record of your thoughts as you read and study. Choose the one that you feel will work best for you. You may want to try a particular method of study for one year and then try another method.

An interesting way to study Psalms or Proverbs, is to rewrite the scriptures yourself, paraphrasing them to apply their truth to your circumstances.

Learn how to mark your Bible. It's okay to write in your Bible! Always remember, the words are sacred, not the pages! Your Bible is your meat, your light, your road map, and so much more. You need a system to be able to find things quickly as you witness and share with others. Write key scriptures in the margins and on the blank pages in the back of the book so you have a personalized "quick reference." You may choose to mark different subjects in different colors: repentance red, baptism blue, and so on, but this isn't necessary. Just don't go overboard, as many new converts do, and highlight every scripture you read! That tends to defeat your purpose!

A complete concordance such as ***Strong's Concordance*** or ***Young's Concordance*** is invaluable when you are trying to locate a particular word or scripture. They list every word in the Bible alphabetically, along with each verse in which the word appears, and it gives the meaning of the word in the language and context that it was originally written in.

You may want to get a Bible Dictionary to help you in your studies. They are very helpful in defining terms that you are unfamiliar with.

A one-volume commentary such as *Matthew Henry's Commentary* would be helpful, as would a Bible Atlas and a book of customs from Bible Days.

Another key to Bible study is to stay in the Bible as much as possible and use the other resources to help you. It is often easy to get sidetracked and spend more time reading the commentaries than you do the Bible. Let the real thing be your primary focus.

How To Study

Prayerfully listen as you read the Bible and God will speak to you. He will reveal the scripture in its historical setting as it related to those in the day it was written and He will reveal its application to you.

As you read, meditate and think on it. Allow it's meaning to mull over in your mind. Write out your thoughts about the meaning and how you can apply it to your life. Memorize a key verse. Ask God to help you apply the scriptures to your life as you ask yourself these questions:

- Is there a sin here for me to confess or avoid?

- Is there a promise to claim and live by?
- Do I need to change an attitude?
- Is there a command to obey?
- Is there an example to follow or avoid?
- Is there something to pray for or praise God about?
- What truth can I learn about God from this passage?

If you will commit to read three chapters a day and five chapters on Sunday, which takes approximately fifteen to twenty minutes, you will read through the Bible in one year! Committing to fifteen minutes and sticking to it is far better than committing to an hour a day and not being able to meet your goal.

After you have read through the Bible completely, you may choose to study a specific book and thoroughly analyze it. By reading through it several times, studying its historical background and picking out major divisions and key phrases, you'll have an in depth understanding of its theme and purpose. The Thompson Chain Reference Bible, mentioned earlier, has an excellent outline and preface to each book of the Bible. It tells who is credited with writing it, the year it was written in and other pertinent material to give in depth understanding as you read.

Perhaps you would like to study the meaning of a particular word. Using a concordance will help you to understand the original meaning of the word in its scriptural context. Old Testament words were originally written in Hebrew. New Testament words were originally written in Greek. Some words have much deeper meanings in their original tongue than the English translation affords them. Love, for instance, in the New Testament, can mean one of three types of love in our language, using the concordance directs your understanding of the true meaning of the word.

Customs from Biblical days are foreign to us. It is interesting to study the culture of the people in relationship to our culture. For example, Jesus told the parable of the woman who lost one of her coins. We may think, "What's the big deal, it's just a coin," but in her culture, its loss represented irresponsibility on her part that was actually grounds for divorce.

Character studies are also interesting to do. When you study the things people did and said, you understand their personality, their relationship to God and their relationship to others. You learn how they reacted when they made mistakes or people "wronged" them. We can learn traits we may wish to imitate and traits we may wish to avoid.

Become a Bible Teacher

Don't keep God's word to yourself! One of the best ways to learn is to teach. Share your excitement and hunger to know God's word with others.

There are many good Bible Studies available that go through the Bible in ten lessons, teaching a basic understanding of Bible chronology, of how the scriptures fit together, and the plan of salvation. ***Search for Truth*** and ***Exploring God's Word*** are two very good studies produced by Word Aflame. These particular Bible studies can be purchased by calling 314-837-7300.

Encourage all new converts to begin reading their Bible right away. To prevent "burn out," steer them away from beginning with Genesis. Have them begin reading the Gospels: Matthew, Mark, Luke and John, so they will understand the Good News of Jesus. Then instruct them to read the book of Acts, the birthplace of the church. Psalms and Proverbs are always great reading for encouragement and wisdom.

An Amazing Book

The Bible is truly an amazing book! I am on my seventh time of reading it through and I am still finding new things! My Pastor/husband has read through the Bible nineteen times and every once in a while, I am able to share something new with him! It never gets old, it never gets stale, it is ***my most prized possession.***

My Most Prized Possession

It's mine, and yet it belongs to all mankind.
It's only four years old, and yet it has always been.
It comes in blue, red, green, black and white.
It is sandwiched between plastic, paper or leather covers.
It's a light and a roadmap to help you find your way when you're lost in the dark.
It can help you climb every mountain and lead you out of every valley.
It's a mirror that allows you to see inside yourself.
It's a laver of cleansing water.
It's milk for some and meat for others.
It's a seed that when planted bears a precious tree of life.
It's sharper than any two-edged sword.
It's been used by kings, presidents, prisoners and paupers alike.
Armies have marched against it and men have tried to destroy it.
It's been chained to desks so the common man would not have access to it.
Once it was lost in a temple for a hundred years.
Some have lived by it; others have died for it.
It took forty men 1600 years to write and yet it has only one author.
It contains sweet love poems and stern letters of reprimand.
It's a book of poetry, songs, riddles, biographies, essays, history and law.
It's really sixty-six separate books under one cover.
It has been translated into more languages than any other book.
It's the most widely read book in history; more copies of it have been printed than any other book.
It's the best selling and least read book in all the world today.

It's a problem solver and has all of the answers to life's
 perplexing problems.
It gives rest when you're weary and trades comfort for pain.
It's the most prized possession I own.
Maybe it's the book you've always meant to read-
 the BIBLE.

                                      Joanne Putnam

Daily Diary

Day: **Date:**

Passage read:

God's message to me today:

A promise:

A command:

A Timeless Principle:

Daily Devotional Journal

Date:

Passage:

1. What questions do I have as a result of reading this passage?

2. What new discoveries did I make today?

3. New ideas about God:

4. New ideas about man:

5. Commands to obey:

6. Promises to claim:

7. Examples to follow or to avoid:

8. Ideas for future study:

9. Notes:

This is the simplest formula I've ever seen but it can be very effective as you reflect on what you read:

Daily Journal

Date:

Passage read:

I learned: (As you read today, what things did you find that were new to you?)

I relearned: (As you read today, what things did you find that you already knew about?)

I still wonder: (After reading today, what questions do I still have regarding this topic?)

Daily Journal

Date:

Scripture Passage:

What does it say?

What does it mean?

What does it men to me?

How will my life be different because I have studied this?

Chapter Seventeen
Spiritual Growth Journal

Do you realize that God used the personal journals of Matthew, Mark, Luke and John to chronicle the earthly life of Jesus in the Gospels? They walked with Him daily. They saw Him perform miracles of healing, feeding thousands of people, casting out demons and preaching to the masses. Without their recordings we wouldn't know about the ten lepers that were cleansed, the widow's son who was raised from the dead, the blind eyes and deaf ears that were opened, or the strong warnings given to the Scribes and Pharisees. These great men described the reactions of the people whose lives were made whole and whose minds were set free. They delivered to us the "Good News" of the Gospel through their writings. They recorded the thoughts, activities and spiritual growth of Jesus.

I would like to encourage you to keep a Spiritual Growth Journal to chronicle *your* spiritual growth. If you truly desire to *grow* in Christ, a journal provides the perfect avenue for recording growth and development. Writing allows you to reflect on what you have done and how you have grown. When you keep a journal, God becomes more personal as you become more aware of His guidance and protection.

The discipline of writing slows you down a bit. It helps you to capture, process and celebrate your journey with God. It gives you a chance to stop and think things through, to treasure and remember the little things that are so quickly forgotten in today's hustle and bustle. When you journal, you can often hear God's voice speaking to you, encouraging you and guiding you. David said, "I will meditate on all your works and consider your mighty deeds" (Psalms 77:12). "Remember the wonders He has done" (Psalms 105:5). God told Jeremiah to "Write thee all the words that I have spoken unto thee in a book" (Jeremiah 30:2).

Journaling helps you to process life. When things happen to you that you just don't understand or feel are unfair; writing them down helps you to take a step back to examine what happened. It acts as a sounding board and provides a safety valve to keep you from lashing out at loved ones in frustration. It helps you organize your thoughts and allows you to see problems differently, more objectively and more positively.

I think of journal writing as "Capturing Your Vapor." James said, "For what is your life? It is even a vapour, that appeareth for a little time, and then vanisheth away." So much happens in life that quickly vanishes if not recorded.

The term "journal" literally comes from the word "journey." In Europe you still see "journeymen." They travel from town to town learning their trade. They work with men who are considered to be experts in their field. As the young men go from one shop to the next, they must record the skills they learn, the tools they operate, the projects they work on, and the things that impress them the most about the "meister."

A journal is meant to record a journey, *your* journey through life. In it you record your thoughts, activities and personal growth as you learn new skills from *the master,* Jesus Christ. It is not meant to be a diary in which you record the minute by minute account of daily happenings.

God **will** speak to you as you write. You may cry, you may laugh or you may just sit in "awe and wonder" as you listen to Him minister to your heart. Days, weeks, months or even years later, when you return to reread the thoughts you wrote, you will be reminded and amazed at the precious times you spent in God's presence. You will recall the peace that reigned in the midst of the storm as you gave your problems to Him. You will recall the special needs He met, the answered prayers and the times when you just shook your head and couldn't believe that even God could have brought situations to pass!

Take time to record the "stuff of life" as well. Compliments you've received, things your children have said, and special times with your spouse are all worth recording.

The only "tools" you need is paper and a writing utensil. You can be as elaborate or simple as you choose to be. If a spiral notebook fits your style, then use a spiral notebook. Just make sure that you consistently write in the same book and that you date each entry.

I would suggest a three-ring binder that has room for dividers. The following are simply suggestions for headings of the sections and their contents:

- Prayer requests and answers to prayer.
- Daily Bible Reading and Study.
- Notes taken on the books you are reading. Record the author and quotes that are important to you. (*Growing In All The Right Places* is the result of many years of note taking and filing of materials on the subject of spiritual growth.)
- Ways in which God has allowed you to minister to and disciple others.
- Steps of faith you have taken that God has honored and rewarded.
- Miracles that have transpired as a result of your walk with God.
- Spiritual goals such as reading through the Bible completely, teaching a Bible Study to a friend, controlling your anger or depression.
- Notes on sermons you've heard. Record the speaker's name, the date and place of the meeting. It may be something you will refer to for years to come.
- Record your thoughts, dreams, relationships, laughter, sorrows, and frustrations and see how God responds to them in time!

I guarantee you that when you make the effort to grow and be accountable to God on a daily basis; He will use you in unbelievable ways. As you experience the trials of life, He is developing skills in you that will be used to minister to the needs of others. He gives you not only the resources to help them, but you will have the "heart" empathy as well.

One author called journaling, "…a fascinating and invaluable history of Christian discovery and healing." To which all I can add is, "Amen!"

Chapter Eighteen
Leaders are Readers

Reading is a *must* if you desire to grow spiritually. *A leader must be a reader and a learner before he is a teacher*! When we read, we find new information that forces us to evaluate ourselves and make necessary changes. Growing spiritually involves change. We do not grow when we maintain the status quo in our lives.

Perhaps some people choose not to read because they don't want to be exposed to new thoughts and ideas. They don't want to be challenged to change. Like the unclean vessel, they would rather let their mind stagnate. When you stop learning how to become more Christ-like, how to minister to the needs of people and how to share the Good News, you stop growing spiritually.

Reading helps us to avoid making the same mistakes others have made. It helps us to deal with situations in our lives that we don't understand. Many books are written as a result of God meeting a particular need in the author's life and their desire to help others to grow spiritually as a result of their trial or test.

Paul said he shared what happened to him so others would understand that tests and trials are normal and that they would get through them if they fainted not.

Eleanor Roosevelt once wrote, "Learn from the mistakes of others. You can't live long enough to make them all yourself."

Inspirational speaker, teacher and writer, Mamie McCullough wrote, "In my life, I've learned a lot of things. Some things I learned the hard way by making mistakes, falling on my face, losing money, and embarrassing myself. Other things I learned the more intelligent way by reading books, listening to cassettes, attending classes, and seeking advice from people smarter than me."

"Where no counsel is, the people fall: but in the multitude of counsellors there is safety" (Proverbs 11:14).

"Without counsel purposes are disappointed: but in the multitude of counsellors they are established" (Proverbs 15:22).

"For by wise counsel thou shalt make thy war: and in multitude of counsellors there is safety" (Proverbs 24:6).

Your primary text should *always* be the Bible, and you should have time set aside to read it daily, but don't stop there. There are many wonderful Christian authors today that share pure Biblical counsel and teaching through their books. At the end of this chapter, you will find the names of several authors and their books. These are books that I have personally read and recommend.

If you have a specific need in your life that you desire to grow in, or a problem that you have been dealing with, choose one of the books from the list and see if it doesn't help to meet that need. Or you may want to ask a trusted friend to suggest a book that will address your individual need.

Before you read a book, pray. Ask God to direct your heart and mind as you read. Ask Him to give you wisdom and to help you glean the kernels of truth that He would have you receive as a result of reading the book. Ask Him to help you apply the truths and principles to your personal life as you seek to grow in Him.

When you read, read with a purpose and read selectively. Not every book is worth your time and energy. There have been many books that I have put down after a few chapters simply because I didn't feel they had the information I needed. Some books may have only a couple of chapters that are of interest to you. Some books may be used simply as reference books to be referred to at a later date as needed. When you read, keep a highlighter, pen and notebook handy. Mark your books so you can retrieve the information later. Make a star or asterisk to denote things that really minister to you as you read. If you are keeping a spiritual growth journal, you might want to jot down some notes in it. Make sure you note the author and title of the book. You never know what God may have planned for you. I never dreamed that notes I took from books I read nearly twenty years ago would be useful in my teaching and ministry today!

Encourage your family to be readers. "Iron sharpeneth iron; so a man sharpeneth the countenance of his friend" (Proverbs 27:17). It is a wonderful experience to share thoughts back and forth as you discuss issues. When you discuss with others what you are learning, you remember it better, you are more apt to apply it to your life and you become the "teacher" as you share ideas and concepts.

If you are not typically a reader, you need to set a personal goal for the year to read at least two books. If you struggle with reading, you may want to get your books on tape so you can listen to them. There are many audio books that will help you grow spiritually.

Joining a Christian book club is a wonderful way to keep up with the latest book offerings. They often have an introductory special where you receive several books for a very minimal price if you agree to purchase a small amount of books within the next year or two. Fliers are sent every month that offer sale prices, new releases and candid descriptions of the books contents. I have used these as guides many times before I purchased a new book. Information on the clubs I would suggest, are listed at the end of the **Authors, Topics & Titles** list.

Authors, Topics & Titles to "Jumpstart" Your Growth

Depression

Tim La Haye *How To Win Over Depression*
Florence Littauer *Blow Away The Black Clouds*
Dr. Frank Minirth/ Dr. Paul Meier *Happiness is a Choice*
The Minirth/Meier Clinic has several books dealing with this issue.

Finances

Ron Blue has many very good books that deal with various aspects of finances.
Larry Burkett *The Financial Planning Workbook, How To Manage Your Money, The Family Budget Workbook, Women Leaving the Workplace*
Amy Dacyczyn *The Tightwad Gazette*
Cheri Fuller *Home Business Happiness*
Mary Hunt *The Complete Cheapskate*

Organization and Personal Management

Emilie Barnes writes on time management and household organization.
More Hours In My Day, Welcome Home, The Fifteen Minute Organizer, Creative Home Organizer
Sandra Felton *The Messies Manuel I and II*
Anne Ortlund *The Disciplines of the Beautiful Woman*
Kathy Peel *The Family Manager*
Quinn Sherrer and Laura Watson *A Christian Woman's Guide to Hospitality*
Pam Young and Peggy Jones *S.H.E. Sidetracked Home Executives*

Relationships

Husband/wife

Sandra P. Aldrich *Men Read Newspapers, Not Minds*
Gary Chapman *The Five Languages of Love*
Linda Dillow *Creative Counterpart*
Dr James Dobson *Straight Talk to Men and Their Wives, What Wives Wish Their Husbands Knew About Women, Love Must Be Tough*
Tim LaHaye *The Act of Marriage, How To Be Happy Though Married, Opposites Attract*
Florence Littauer *After Every Wedding Comes a Marriage*
Rev. John Maxwell *Becoming a Person of Influence, Developing the Leader Within You*
Marabel Morgan *The Total Woman*
John Trent, Ph.D. *Life Mapping*
Gary Smalley *The Language of Love*
Ed Wheat M.D. *Intended For Pleasure*
Dr. H. Norman Wright *How To Really Love Your Wife, How To Really Love Your Husband*

Children

Dr. Kevin Leman *Making Kids Mind Without Loosing Yours, Bringing Up Your Kids Without Tearing Them Down, The Birth Order Book, Unlocking the Secrets of Your Childhood Memories*
Dr. James Dobson *Dare to Discipline, Hide and Seek, Emotions, Can You Trust Them, Parenting Isn't for Cowards,* and many others
June Hines Moore *You Can Raise a Well-mannered Child*
Gary Smalley and John Trent *The Blessing*

Spiritual Growth/Encouragement

Patsy Clairmont *Sport'in a 'Tude*
Focus on the Family *Seven Promises of a Promise Keeper*
Tim La Haye *The Spirit-Controlled Temperament*
Melva Lea *Desperate Women, Praying Through Life's Problems*
Florence Littauer *Silver Boxes, Personality Plus, It Takes So Little To Be Above Average, The Personality Puzzle, Getting Along With Almost Anybody*
Jean Lush *Emotional Phases of a Woman's Life, Women and Stress*
Joyce Meier *Me and My Big Mouth*
Dr Frank Minirth/ Dr. Paul Meier   (Minirth/Meier Clinic) *The Anger Workbook, Happiness is a Choice* and many more.
Robert Mc Gee *The Search for Significance*

Christian Book Clubs

Crossings
6550 E. 30th Street
PO Box 6325
Indianapolis, IN 46206-6325

Pentecostal Book Club
8855 Dunn Road
Hazelwood, MO 63042-2299

Chapter Nineteen
For Those Tears

Have you ever wondered why you cry? Have you ever felt like you would never quit crying? Or are you one of those people who wishes they could cry?

Tears have always been important to God, so much so, that people felt that they should save them in the hope that some day they would formally present them to their maker.

In many of the ancient Jewish tombs, little glass vials have been found. They are approximately one inch wide and three to five inches long. Research has shown that these little bottles, sometimes made of alabaster, once held the tears of loved ones who mourned over their death, as well as their own tears, which were to be presented to God as proof of their worship and sacrifice to Him.

Tears are quite interesting. They are made of a salt-water solution and come from little ducts tucked into the corner of the eye. Tears continually bathe the cornea. They help to clear it of foreign particles such as dust and hairs and keep it from drying out, which would result in blindness. Though mostly a salt solution, tears contain substances that fight bacteria, and proteins that help keep the eye immune to infection. You know from, experience that if you get something in your eye, it immediately closes and tears begin to flow. Tears wash out the foreign object.

Tears do more than bring physical healing to our eyes. Tears bring release, healing and freedom to our soul, if we would just allow them to! Tears come when we show compassion, love, joy and sorrow. We shed them in happy times and in sad times. Sadly, there are times in our lives when we are extremely heavy hearted; yet we hold back from God our true feelings, failing to release them to Him. We refuse to give our tears to Him.

All too often we see men, who from a child, have been told, "Boys don't cry, only sissies cry." So they hold feelings and hurts so tightly on the inside that it turns into bitterness and hardness of heart that can ultimately destroy them.

In Psalm 56: 8 & 9, we find David calling out to God. "Thou tellest my wanderings: put thou my tears into thy bottle: are they not in thy book. When I cry unto thee, then shall mine enemies turn back: this I know; for God is for me." David was asking God to put his tears in a bottle and record them in His book.

Hezekiah received a word from the Lord as a result of his tears. "I have heard thy prayer, I have seen thy tears: behold, I will heal thee…" (2 Kings 20:5).

Isaiah, seeking the Lord in 16:9 says, "Therefore, will I bewail with the weeping… I will water thee with tears…."

Job mentions over and over his weeping before the Lord. Job 16:20 says, "My friends scorn me: but mine eye poureth out tears unto God." Apparently, even in Job's day, it was disdainful (beneath one's dignity) for a man to cry.

One of the most precious scriptures, so very short but eternally deep, is John 11:35, "Jesus wept." Many feel that Jesus wept, not because of the death of Lazarus, but rather the unbelief of those He loved that did not understand what He was really telling them. Jesus experienced the same frustrations that we experience; and He expressed them in the same way we do.

Just as Job was scorned for weeping, the Lord was also treated with contempt one day. He was invited to eat at a certain Pharisees house. They had just sat down to eat, when a woman of the city, a sinner, came to the house and stood at Jesus' feet, weeping.

She then knelt before Him and began to wash His feet with her tears. In the fact that she was literally "washing His feet with her tears," she must have been using more than the tears shed in weeping. I believe she was pouring out her vials of tears upon her God's feet, not wanting to wait until she died to present them to Him in the next life. Luke says she wiped Jesus' feet with the hairs of her head and anointed them with precious ointment from an alabaster box.

Those around Him scorned this woman of the city found to be a sinner and in their hearts they hated Jesus for allowing this "shameful" act to take place.

Jesus understood both her humbleness and her sacrifice. He immediately forgave her sins, telling her that her faith had saved her and to go in peace. He then rebuked the Pharisees, for they had not even followed the common courtesy of giving Him water to wash His feet nor had they anointed His head with oil, which was customary to bestow upon every male guest who entered your home. He extolled to them the humbleness of this woman, who washed His feet with her tears, dried them with her hair and anointed His feet with ointment when they couldn't bring themselves to anoint His head. She truly had given her all to the Lord.

When we approach God, in humbleness of heart, He hears us and will accomplish that which we have need of. Answers come. Healing comes. Salvation comes.

"The righteous cry, and the Lord heareth, and delivereth them out of all their troubles. The Lord is nigh unto them that are of a broken heart; and saveth such as be of a contrite spirit" (Psalms 34:17, 18).

"For thou has delivered my soul from death, mine eyes from tears." (Psalms 116:8).

"They that sow in tears shall reap in joy. He that goeth forth and weepeth, bearing precious seed, shall doubtless come again with rejoicing, bringing his sheaves with him" (Psalm126: 5,6).

"Weeping endureth for a night. But joy cometh in the morning" (Psalm 30:5).

Paul told the New Testament church that he shed many tears in prayer and supplication for them. Evidently it was not beneath his dignity.

Soon there will come a day when tears shall be no more: "And God shall wipe away all tears from their eyes; and there shall be no more death, neither sorrow, nor crying, neither shall there be any more pain..." (Revelations 21:4).

Until our tears are taken away, God has given us a release valve that allows us to cleanse our soul, to minister to others and to show compassion. We may not collect them and put them in bottles, but God sees them none the less and is recording them in His book, the ***Lamb's Book of Life***!

Chapter Twenty

Image Makers

Today we have "Image Makers." If you don't like who you are or what you look like, a consultant can *make you over*. They'll change your hairstyle, your hair color and your makeup. They'll design a diet and exercise program to change your figure. They'll consult clothing styles and color charts to assure you of the perfect hues to compliment your hair color and facial tones. They'll walk you through charm school and teach you the latest etiquette, but the *real you* will still be inside.

They may have the ability to change the outside appearance, but the inside remains the same. The *real you* is what God sees. The *real you* is the person that He wants to see. You are a woman by God's design. He has a distinct plan and purpose for your life.

Today's women face tremendous pressures and responsibilities. They are only one person, but bear the responsibility of many more. They are expected to get a good education, enter a profitable full-time career, marry, have 1.4 perfect children, homeschool, keep their home like "House Beautiful," cook like Susie Gourmet, run errands, grocery shop, shuttle children to every event, be president of the local parent teacher organization and stay fresh and happy while doing it all!

Unfortunately, it doesn't work quite that way, at least not for long. Many women experience burnout. They feel inadequate when they can't live up to the Super Mom image. Often they end up with a poor self-image and depression. They don't know who they are; and they are unsure as to who they're supposed to be.

The world screams at women through every avenue of the media to be something other than what God designed them to be. The world tells them to be tough, but God tells them to be tender. The world tells them to stand up for their rights, God says that vengeance is His and that He will fight your battles for you.

You must realize that God has His own design and plan for your life. When you truly submit yourself to Him, He makes you in His image!

When we worked with the military in Germany, we saw many beautiful young ladies who had joined the Army simply to prove that they were *just as tough as the guys.* They found though, that when they came to God and desired to know Him in the light of His Word, that their former desires changed. A transformation took place as they became a new creature in Christ Jesus. They soon realized that God didn't create them to be *one of the guys*. He created them to be entirely different! As they grew spiritually, their entire self-image changed. They felt the confidence they needed to become the special person that God intended them to be, A Woman!

When you come to God and allow His precious Spirit to soften your heart, you become *radiantly beautiful* in Him. It doesn't matter that your nose is too big or your ears stick out. It doesn't matter that you don't have the most up-to-date wardrobe. You are an individual with special talents and abilities that He desires to develop in you for use in His kingdom. He desires that you grow in Him.

God's primary concern is that your spirit be right. This is where He values *beauty*. When your spirit is right, it seeps into your whole being and overflows into the lives of others. Jesus said that He came that we might have life, and life more abundantly (John 10:10). When we allow Christ to be our image-maker, we become like Him. Our life takes on new meaning and we enjoy it to the fullest.

We make our own choice. We can choose to go through life with a mask on our soul that is seen and acknowledged by those we meet, never really experiencing all that God has for us. Or we can choose to live life in the fullest, not only here on earth, but for all eternity.

Perhaps you don't really know where you stand with God. You think you are a Christian but you are struggling with things that you know are not pleasing to God. If this is you, take time right now to commit your life to God.

Ask Him to help you to be real with yourself and real with Him. Ask Jesus to help you to grow into His image of you.

Romans 3:23 tells us that *"all have sinned and come short of the glory of God."* We must acknowledge the fact that we are a sinner in need of a savior.

The next step is repentance. Repentance is a turning away from sin. It is humbling yourself before God and asking for His forgiveness for the things that you have done that are not pleasing in His sight.

On the very first day of the church, known as the day of Pentecost, (Acts 2), Peter, to whom Jesus had given the keys of the kingdom of heaven, boldly stood up and preached. At the end of his message, the scripture says, "Now when they heard this they were pricked in their heart, and said unto Peter and to the rest of the apostles, men and brethren, what shall we do?" (Acts 2:37). (They were asking, "What do we need to do to be saved?")

"Then Peter said unto them, Repent and be baptized every one of you in the name of Jesus Christ for the remission of sin, and ye shall receive the gift of the Holy Ghost. For the promise is unto you and to your children, and to all that are afar off, even as many as the Lord our God shall call" (Acts 2:38, 39).

If you follow the plan that Peter set forth on the first day of the church, you will know where you stand with God and you can begin the awesome journey of growing in Him. Receiving the Baptism of the Holy Spirit, (with the evidence of speaking with other tongues, as the scripture says) is what gives you the power to live holy before God. The same Spirit that created the universe and penned the scriptures becomes resident in your heart and soul. Scriptures come alive as you read them with more understanding.

God created you in His image and likeness. He has a specific plan and purpose for your life. You are a woman by God's design. Allow Him to mold you and make you into the ***Vessel of Honor*** that He desires you to be.

For further information, or if you would like to order the six page *Personality Profile*, additional copies of ***Growing in All the Right Places***, or teaching tapes, please contact:

Joanne Putnam
PO Box 123
Monroe, WI 53566

Growing in All the Right Places	$11.00
Personality Profile (by Fred Littauer)	$ 1.00

Cassette Tapes:
Understanding The Personalities $ 5.00
    Speaker: Joanne Putnam
For Bitter or Better $5.00
    Speaker: Joanne Putnam

Shipping:
$1.50 for each book, profile, or cassette.

Sales Tax:
Please add 5% for books shipped to Wisconsin addresses.